Maine Ghosts and Legends

Maine Ghosts and Legends

26 Encounters with the Supernatural

Thomas A. Verde

Down East Books • Camden, Maine

Book design by Lurelle Cheverie
Composition by High Resolution, Inc. Camden, Maine
Printed and bound at Banta Company, Harrisonburg, Virginia

4 5

Down East Books
Camden, Maine

This book is lovingly dedicated
To my nephews and nieces,
Who all enjoy a good ghost story

Contents

Haunted Places and Objects

Haunted Inns and Taverns

Preface

This book has its origins in a week-long series of narrated ghost stories I produced for the Maine Public Broadcasting Network's radio news show "Maine Things Considered" in the autumn of 1986. In the course of doing my research for the series, I made two very interesting discoveries. One, that Maine was rich in ghost stories and legends; two, that there is no single book dedicated solely to the state's supernatural heritage. Thus, I decided to write one.

I didn't really believe strongly in the existence of spirits when I started this project. I had heard stories here and there, but didn't give them very much thought. If I had, I may have come to believe in these things earlier. During the writing of this book I heard dozens of ghost stories, usually recounted for me by eye witnesses, and I noted several startlingly common elements in these testimonies. These include fluctuating room temperatures (either very hot or very cold), the sensitivity of animals and children to spiritual entities, unaccountable sounds, such as of water pouring, bumps and knocks, and, lastly, the simple sensation that there was just another "presence" in the house or room.

Different combinations of these elements appear again and again in these stories. They have been related by persons from all over the state who, to the best of my knowledge, have never met each other and thus have had no occasion to collude in some sort of grand fraud. The fact remains that these events recur with uncanny frequency in many of these stories.

Some theorize that ghosts are merely imprints left upon the fabric of the present by intense individual experiences or events in the past. We view them as we would the characters in an old motion picture that is played over and over again even though the actors actually died long ago. Psychics often speak in terms of "energy" when they refer to ghosts, and of how spirits are nothing more than the residual energy left in a room or a place where a person had once lived and been happy—or sad.

My own research, plus reading I have done on the topic of mysticism, compels me to think that ghosts are as much a part of our reality as we believe our own souls to be. We cannot physically touch the soul, yet many of us accept that it exists. To be less mystical about it, only under certain conditions can we see, hear, or feel electricity, yet we certainly believe in its existence. So too with ghosts. Under certain conditions, and to certain people, they make themselves known.

I have accepted the testimonies of the people in this book as truth. You will have to judge for yourself.

THOMAS A. VERDE
Portland, Maine

There are more things in heaven and earth, Horatio,
Than are dreamt of in your philosophy.

HAMLET ACT I, SCENE 5

Ghost Legends

1

The Flying Dutchman of Maine

S he was one of the swiftest ships of her kind in that day. She had made journeys from Portland and Freeport to Port au Prince, Bermuda, and the Carolinas and back, unharmed and laden with barrels of coffee, hogsheads of rum, lumber, rice, flour, and other goods. She had procured this bounty through the privateering of British ships during the War of 1812, a conflict that inspired the building of a great many American schooners with the primary function of harassing and outrunning the English navy up and down the eastern seaboard.

Her name was *Dash*, and she had been commissioned in June of 1812 to "detain, seize and take all vessels to whomsoever belonging," along with their goods and crews and bring them into U.S. ports for legal prosecution "under the rights of the United States as a power at war." The *Dash* was a Freeport ship. Her modified mainmast afforded her more sail and hence extra speed, and her hull was soaped and tallowed to reduce the build-up of barnacles and weeds, lending her further swiftness. She had been built at Porter's Landing and was owned by the Porter brothers: William, of Portland, and Samuel, of Freeport. Manned primarily by Freeport sailors, the *Dash* distinguished herself in the war by repeated victorious encounters with the enemy British ships and by her successful transportation of goods from southern ports back to Maine.

For three years, under the command of a variety of captains, the *Dash* made fifteen voyages along the coast with minimal damage and loss of life. The memory of the *Dash* and her outstanding maritime achievements would, no doubt, have lived on in American naval history even without the tragic addendum to her story that marked her sixteenth and final voyage out of Portland.

It was on a cold day in late January of 1815 that the *Dash* and one of her sister ships, the *Chamberlain*, set sail, encountering a gale after two days at sea. The *Chamberlain* changed course, but the *Dash* drove on into the storm, disappearing from sight—but not, some will avow, forever Only months later some fishermen in Casco Bay swore to hearing a vessel bearing down on them out of the mists and suddenly seeing a phantom ship glide by them through the fog, bound for Freeport. On her bow were inscribed the words "Dash—Freeport."

The incidence of sightings by fishermen and other boaters on the bay increased over the years. Although the ghost ship would appear seemingly at random, certain details were noted at each instance—there would always be a fog up; there would be no breeze, even though the ship would be cruising fast, as it had been known to during its earthly service at sea; and the crew would be seen standing on the bow, their eyes toward Freeport. The legend of the *Dash* grew, and soon it was speculated that whenever a family member of one of the lost sixty crewmen died, the ship would return from the hereafter to bear the loved one on board for the final journey.

It would seem that the last occurrence of such a death took place during the early days of World War II when the U.S. Navy was guarding the waters of Casco Bay. According to an account by journalist Henry Paper published by *Greater Portland* magazine in 1985, one foggy afternoon a blip appeared on the radar screen, right in the middle of the protected waters. As sirens went off and all hands were called to their stations, the Coast Guard and the Navy swept in upon what appeared to be the unbelievable—it was the *Dash*. Cruising along its usual course, through the fog and bound for Freeport, the *Dash* made its way up the channel. By the time the surprised armed ships were ready to converge on the phantom boat, it had disappeared. The incident has gone down in the annals of World War II as one of the most bizarre occurrences of that conflict.

Will we ever see the *Dash* again? According to legend, this will depend on how many descendents of its crew are still alive today or, more specifically, when they die. It is, of course, possible that the legend of the *Dash* is simply that—a tale spun by superstitious seamen of another time; then again, perhaps Maine's own *Flying Dutchman* took on the last of her crewmembers during a foggy afternoon in the 1940s. The best advice one can offer is to keep your eyes peeled and your ears cocked when a sudden fog embraces the bay, and recall the fate of the *Dash* as one local poet, Elisa Dennison King, did when she wrote:

> You have heard of the ship that sails the bay,
> With night for a helmsman and death in tow,
> And that glides to sea as he comes ashore
> And speeds on his errand of woe . . .
>
> But when any of those who loved the lads
> Are ready to slip their moorings here

And sail away to the unknown port
You will see the Dead Ship gliding near.

"And the ship and the life go out with the tide"
And the Captain paused for a while then said
"They are most all gone and the Dead Ship soon
Will come no more for the souls of the dead."

—QUOTED IN *THREE CENTURIES OF FREEPORT, MAINE*,
BY FLORENCE G. THURSTON

2

The Curse
of the
Saco River

The Saco River, one of Maine's largest, has its origins in the White Mountains and winds its way across the southern corner of the state to empty into the Atlantic at Ferry Beach and beautiful Biddeford Pool. The Saco has long been a source of enjoyment for fishermen, canoeists, and swimmers from Fryeburg to Camp Ellis. Yet until as recently as 1947, some Maine folks in the Saco-Biddeford area would hesitate to go near the waters of the Saco until they were certain that three people had drowned there that season. Their fears stemmed from a centuries-old curse placed upon the Saco by an Indian chief—a curse that demanded the lives of three white men every year. This is its story.

The early English settlers in Maine were not always welcomed by the Native Americans who resided there. The exception to this rule was the white settlement at Winter Harbor near present-day Saco and Biddeford. Here the English encountered a friendly tribe called the Sokokis (hence the *Saco* River), with whom they engaged in trade and lived peacefully for half a century. That peace was shattered, however, in the summer of 1675.

In the spring and summer, the Sokokis enjoyed the pleasant retreat of Factory Island, then a beautifully wooded isle in the Saco several miles in from the coast. Here they hunted, fished, and swam in the cool, foaming waters of the cataracts that flowed down each side and emptied into the bay. One of the most respected leaders of the Sokokis was a chief named Squando. Not only a great sachem, Squando was supposed to have commanded the powers of sorcery and magic. Dignified and solemn, Squando was respected among the whites as well for the peace he maintained with them. Legend had it that he once returned a little white girl who had been captured in an Indian raid years before and reared by the Sokokis. In the early months of the destructive King Philip's War, it was Squando who kept the peace between his tribe and the English, while other New England tribes were readying themselves for battle. Squando's heart was turned against the whites, however, because of a cruel joke.

In the summer of 1675, an English vessel lay at anchor near the mouth of the Saco. Three sailors from the ship rowed up the river and came upon the Indian settlement at Factory Island, then known as Indian Island. They noted a young Indian woman crossing the channel in a canoe. With her was her infant son.

"I have heard," said one sailor, "that these Indian brats can swim at birth, like a very duck or dog or beaver."

"What say you?" laughed another. "Let us find out."

The sailors blocked the Indian woman's way in the channel and tore the screaming infant from her arms. While one held her back, the other threw the helpless child overboard, where it immediately sank in the river. The mother broke free and dove in after the baby. She rescued him, but he soon fell ill and died. The sailors, thinking it all a fine joke, rowed back to their ship, unaware of what they had done. They did not know that this Indian woman was no ordinary squaw, but the wife of a great sagamore; they were further unaware that this little baby they had, in effect, killed was Menewee, the son of Squando.

For three days and nights, Squando mourned at the grave of Menewee, while:

> In his wigwam, still as stone
> [Sat] a woman all alone,
>
> Wampum beads and birchen strands
> Dropping from her careless hands
> Listening ever for the fleet
> Patter of a dead child's feet.

FROM "THE TRUCE OF PISCATAQUA," BY JOHN GREENLEAF WHITTIER

On the third day, Squando went down to the river and stood on its banks with his arms outstretched. He cursed the waters of the Saco and vowed revenge upon the whites who had killed his son. He commanded the spirits of the river to take the lives of three white men every year until they were driven from "Saco's hemlock-trees."

He then went among the Sokokis and fueled the fires of their resentment toward the white settlers, and it was here in Saco that the first major blow of the King Philip's War was struck.

Squando's curse was fulfilled each year until the mid 1940s, when a year passed with no drownings and the *Maine Sunday Telegram* headline happily proclaimed, "Saco River Outlives Curse of Indian Chief." Although years after Menewee's drowning Squando was supposed to have made his peace with the whites, his curse was so feared and respected that for centuries Saco mothers would not allow their children to swim in the river until three white men had drowned there that season.

3

One Foot on
the Grave

I t isn't hard to find. In fact, you can just see it as you cross
the Verona Island bridge heading north on Route 1 into
Bucksport. On a stately rise, anachronistically perched opposite a mini-shopping complex and parking lot, stands the tall,
obelisk-topped tombstone of Colonel Jonathan Buck.

Surrounded by the more diminutive gravestones of his
wife and descendents, the monument to Colonel Buck doesn't
seem to be very much out of the ordinary—an appropriate trib-
ute to the founder of this mid-coast port town and hero of the
Revolutionary War. But when you get a little closer, you can
detect an oddity on the otherwise blank face of granite below
the large, chiseled name of Buck. It's a curious mark, about two
feet long and six inches across at its widest point—a mark that
is black and in the unmistakable shape of a leg and foot from
the knee down. How and why it got there has been an issue of
debate for many years in the town of Bucksport, but most local
residents, if asked about the stone, would shrug their shoul-

ders casually and answer you thus: a witch left the mark there over two hundred years ago, and it has been there ever since.

As with many figures from history, chroniclers have paid more homage to the legends surrounding the man than to the actual facts of his life. History does tell us that Jonathan Buck was born in February of 1719 in Woburn, Massachusetts, and that four years later his family moved to Haverhill, where he spent his boyhood. It wasn't until some forty years later that Buck, then a modestly prosperous shipbuilder and merchant, joined a group of settlers from Massachusetts and New Hampshire and petitioned the Massachusetts Court (Maine was then still part of Massachusetts and didn't become independent until 1820) for certain parcels of land in the area of the Penobscot River.

This territory had just been wrested from the French and opened for settlement by the British, who built a fort not far from Bucksport in what is now Stockton Springs. The fort was named Pownal, after a governor of Massachusetts, and Jonathan Buck was to become its last Colonial commander.

Colonel Buck's grandson, Rufus Buck, has left us perhaps the most accurate description of Bucksport's founder. He was "spare, thin . . . with an expressive face, Roman nose, black arching eyebrows, and dark, penetrating eyes." It was said that Colonel Buck was a man of strong convictions and an "iron will, not easily changed." One poet who wrote about Buck and the legend of his gravestone was Robert P. Tristram Coffin, who said of the colonel:

> The King's word was the colonel's word
> The colonel gave the law,
> The colonel's name was on the town
> And all the fields he saw.

FROM: *COLLECTED POEMS OF ROBERT P. TRISTRAM COFFIN*,
(NEW YORK: MACMILLAN CO., 1948)

When war inevitably broke out between the colonists and

Britain, Buck was appointed Colonel of the Fifth Militia Regiment of Lincoln County as well as Justice of the Peace. He was given command of Fort Pownal, although it had been rendered powerless by the British who had carted away the guns and ammunition in 1775. Still, Colonel Buck was an important military leader who in 1779 refused to swear loyalty to the British throne and was eventually forced to flee Bucksport, making his way on foot to the safety of Haverhill.

After the war, Buck and many of the other original settlers returned to Bucksport to resume their lives of commercial prosperity, and the colonel lived to a remarkable seventy-seven years of age, dying in March of 1795. A little more than fifty years after his death, his descendents erected near his gravesite the stone monument that was to become the topic of such wonderment and debate.

There are several versions of the story of how the foot came to appear on the face of the granite monument to Jonathan Buck. However varied and fantastic some are, they all share a common theme: the condemnation of an innocent and the resultant curse brought upon the Bucks in the form of the disfigured gravestone.

It seems that a young woman (whom Coffin in his poem identified as "Ann Harraway") was accused of witchcraft and brought before the colonel for judgment. Although one Bucksport historian, Blakely B. Babcock, points out that the heyday of witch trials in New England had ended a hundred years prior to that, it is apparent that the woman was accused in one way or another of a crime that was punishable by either hanging or burning. The accused had to face the stern and immovable judgment of Colonel Buck, and she was indeed condemned to death. As she was either having the noose placed around her throat or having the flames stoked beneath her feet (depending on which version you prefer), the accused woman was said to have glared down at the colonel and pronounced this curse*:

"Jonathan Buck, listen to these words, the last my
tongue shall utter. In the spirit of the only true and living God I speak to you. You will soon die. Over your
grave they will erect a stone that all may know where
the bones of the mighty Jonathan Buck are crumbling to
dust. But listen, all ye people and may your descendents ever know the truth. Upon that stone will appear
the imprint of my foot, and for all time long after your
accursed race has perished from the earth the people
will come from afar to view the fulfillment and will say:
'There lies the man who murdered a woman.'
Remember well, Jonathan Buck. Remember well!"

After the colonel's death, a normal stone was placed over
his grave with nothing more on it than the usual biographical
information and a brief verse testifying to the passage of the
flesh. It wasn't until 1852, when Buck's descendents decided to
erect a larger memorial to their honorable forebear, that the
witch's curse seemed to come true.

It was noted that the massive piece of granite the family
had selected had been especially chosen for its clean, unblem-
ished surface. Thus it was no doubt with great surprise that
some citizens of the town noticed one morning the clear, dark
image of a foot besmirching the simple face of the monument.
Now the family members thought that some enemy of
theirs—or perhaps some vandals—had committed this out-
rage, and they immediately had the foot washed off with sand,
pumice, and water. This purging lasted for only a few days,
however, because the foot returned in all its simplistic
mockery. Stronger cleansing agents were applied, and they
even tried gouging out the stone's surface, but the mark
returned.

Some people in Bucksport will tell you that the entire monument was replaced once and that the foot returned to the very
same spot on the new monument; others will say that the mon-

ument was never replaced and that the foot is simply an imperfection in the stone known as an inclusion, or knot. If this last assessment is true, however, why didn't the stonemasons notice it originally? Inclusions are readily apparent when the stone is cut; they do not gradually bleed through the rock.

Another question that comes to mind is, why a leg and foot? Chroniclers of the legend have tackled this question in different ways. One relates that it was not a woman who was condemned but a local simpleton, used for a scapegoat in the mysterious murder of a woman whose mutilated body was missing one leg. The poor condemned man was said to have claimed just before his death that the injustice of Colonel Buck and his court would be evidenced by the appearance of the murdered woman's missing leg on the grave.

Perhaps the most romanticized version of the legend comes to us from the pen of the aforementioned Robert P. Tristram Coffin, who conspicuously substituted a T for a B in his poem, "The Foot of Tucksport." Coffin asserts that the witch Ann Harraway had actually been a paramour of Colonel Buck (or Jethro Tuck as Coffin renames him, perhaps recalling one of his own Puritan ancestors, Jethro Coffin) and bore a son by him out of wedlock. This son was a horrid-looking, simian creature who lived with his mother, like *Beowulf*'s Grendel and his witch-parent (possibly where Coffin got the inspiration for this part of his plot), far outside the boundaries of the town on the dark edge of the woods. Despite his ugliness, Colonel Buck's bastard was supposed to have had the same dark brow and hair as his stern father. Coffin goes on to relate that the colonel attempted to bribe Harraway into leaving the area but she refused. After that she was brought before the local church magistrate and Colonel Buck himself, who heard witnesses testifying to her evildoings as a witch. She was sentenced to be burned, and as she was being engulfed by the flames her son suddenly appeared and grasped one of her burning legs from her body. Clasping the leg to his heart, he ran back into the forest, never to be seen again. In Coffin's version, the image of the leg, which "no scrubbing could erase," appears on Buck's grave within days of his burial.

Although Coffin's account is highly embellished, it raises an interesting question that throws a perhaps dishonorable light on the memory of the revered founder of Bucksport. Did Buck have some illicit dealings with a person Coffin characteristically refers to as the "Red Whore of Babylon"? If there was some sort of connection between Buck and a disreputable personage of the time, greater significance might be read into the Buck family's indignation at the appearance of the foot on the monument of their otherwise noble scion.

History gives us no indication that any such tryst existed outside of Coffin's poem, but one fact is certain—if you do go to Bucksport you can see the image of the foot on the colonel's grave. It has been there for over a hundred years, repeated cleansings and skepticism notwithstanding, and it will probably be there for yet another hundred and longer, or, as Coffin puts it:

> Two hundred Winters have not washed
> The [B]ucksport stain away,
> The foot is on the colonel's grave
> Till the Judgement Day.

* This wording for the curse is taken from "The Witch's Curse Fulfilled," *Sun-Up* Magazine 7 (Jan. 1929), p. 12.

4

The Haunted Isles

Lonely, cast-off orphans in the sea, the Isles of Shoals have long been symbols of self-reliance. A scattering of eighteen rocks and islands some six to ten miles off Portsmouth, New Hampshire, the Shoals were probably first visited during the late sixteenth or early seventeenth centuries by fishermen in search of better waters. The islands were first mapped and charted in 1614 by the famous English explorer Captain John Smith, who wrote: "[O]f all the foure parts of the world that I have yet seene not inhabited, could I have but means to transport a Colonie, I would rather live here than any where."

Captain Smith's enthusiasm for the islands was shared by subsequent explorers and fishermen who settled on the various bits of earth and rock that make up the Shoals—Appledore, Star and Smuttynose being among the most popular. Although the inhabitants have always been fiercely independent, their islands are actually divided between two states—New Hampshire and Maine. (Appledore, Smuttynose, Malaga, Cedar, and Duck islands are all in Maine waters.) The people who lived there year-round, however, never considered themselves to be anything else but "Shoalers." Indeed, in the early eighteenth century, one of the selectmen from the Shoals rowed over to Portsmouth to ask officials there if he and his island neighbors might be excused from paying taxes since the New Hampshire town provided no services to them in the way of roads, schools, or police protection. His request was granted.

The Shoalers lived a sober, industrious life on their sundry outposts, and by the mid-nineteenth century were suffering the intrusion of tourists and summer folk during the warm months of the year. As might be expected, they eked out a good part of their living from the sea, and fishing was a thriving industry. Fishermen and traders from as far away as Spain and as close as Boston visited the Shoals to share in the bounty. Many of the boats from Boston were known as "Guinea boats," because they were often crewed by Italians or Portuguese. They were a common sight in the harbors of the Shoals until a tragedy occurred in the early 1900s—a tragedy that became one of the most gruesome ghost tales of the islands.

It seems that one of the crew of a Guinea boat drank a little too much wine one night and went ashore to look for trouble. He found it in the wife of a Shoaler fisherman. He accosted the woman, whose husband was away fishing, and tried to rape her. When she resisted, he killed her with a knife and then hurried back to his vessel. The ship sailed for Boston the next morning and the criminal got away.

When the Shoaler fisherman returned home, he found to his horror that his wife was dead and he was being accused of the murder. The police arrested him and were going to take him to the mainland when a storm came up. They decided to wait it out overnight and stayed in the fisherman's hut, standing guard over their innocent prisoner. In the middle of the night, while the storm raged, the fisherman escaped through a window and made it to the beach, where he got into a dory and set off into the turbulent waters. No one could say for certain if he was ever seen again. He was, however, heard from.

Not long after, during the middle of a foggy night in the Shoals, an agonized scream was heard coming from the fo'c'sle of a Guinea boat. As the boat's crew and other nearby Guinea boaters rushed to the rescue, some thought they heard the sounds of oars being set into tholepins and a boat pulling away. One even believed he saw a figure rowing quickly into the enveloping fog. When they got to the fo'c'sle, they were horrified to find one of their compatriots lying there with his right hand cut off. Guinea-boaters were a tightly knit group. This was the same man, they knew, who had killed the fisherman's wife. They were convinced that the wretched fisherman had come back to take his revenge.

Apparently, though, the fisherman's revenge didn't stop with this one act. The crews of the Guinea boats were consistently attacked for almost twenty years in the middle of foggy or stormy nights. Eyes would be gouged, ears and noses or other appendages would be cropped off, and always someone would hear the sound of the oars or perhaps see the ghostly shape of the fisherman as he disappeared into the night. It became such a plague that the Guinea boats eventually stopped coming to the Isles altogether out of utter fear.

Another tale of ghosts and knives concerns the spirit of one Philip Babb, an early settler and constable for the islands. In addition to his official duties, Babb ran a tavern and a butcher shop on Appledore. Wielding a heavy, sharp blade and wearing a butcher's apron, Babb would slaughter hogs near a cove on Appledore that eventually came to be named after him. He died in 1671 a wealthy and, one would assume, relatively contented man.

However, according to the island's most celebrated historian, Celia Thaxter, Babb was a "desperately wicked" man for whom there was "no rest . . . in his grave." He was rumored to have been one of Captain Kidd's men, and it was firmly believed by the islanders that his ghost haunted the cove bearing his name. Even Nathaniel Hawthorne, in *The American*

Note-Books, wrote of Babb as "Old Babb, the ghost . . . a luminous appearance about him as he walks, and his face . . . pale and very dreadful."

A story goes that one night an islander was rounding the corner of his workshop when he suddenly saw a crazed man running toward him. He first thought that a friend was trying to play a joke on him, so he stood still and waited for the figure to come closer. When it did, the islander saw that the man's ghastly face had the sunken eyes of a corpse. The fiendish figure pulled a long, sharp knife from its belt and wielded it in the poor islander's face. The Shoaler ran screaming all the way to his house, where he found the man he had originally thought was playing a joke on him calmly eating his supper.

On another occasion, an islander was sitting on the porch of his home one warm spring night. Looking toward Babb's Cove, he thought he saw a figure skulking about the rocky beach. The figure then began to make its way toward the path to the islander's house. The islander thought it strange that he hadn't heard any footsteps on the stony beach and rose from his chair to intercept the mysterious form. As he got closer, he was horrified to see the vacant eyes and glowing frock of Babb's ghost. He called out, asking what the ghost wanted, but Babb still advanced, his figure waxing and waning in distinction, until suddenly he just disappeared.

Perhaps the most romantic ghost legend of the Shoals is that of the pirate bride. The Shoals have a long history of being frequented by pirates, and it was said that the Shoalers welcomed them as friends. These marauders didn't go there to raid but to hide out and, some say, bury their stolen treasure. One companion of the bloodthirsty Edward "Blackbeard" Teach, a pirate by the name of Scot, was supposed to have buried a vast treasure on Appledore. When he left on his next pirating voyage, he made his young bride swear that she would stay behind on the island and guard his treasure. The pirate never returned to the Shoals.

Two centuries later, a summer vacationer on the Shoals found the islands so agreeable that he stayed on into the fall. One clear and calm autumn morning, the man was walking along the cliffs at Appledore, gazing out at the sea. Suddenly, he sensed that there was a person standing near him. He turned to see a beautiful young woman wrapped in a dark cloak with long, blonde hair flowing over her shoulders. Like him, she was gazing out at the sea but with an intensity that took the vacationer by surprise. He thought that she must be the wife of some fisherman and asked her casually if there was any sign of "him," meaning her fisherman husband. She turned and looked at him with, as Thaxter writes, "the largest and most melancholy blue eyes" and said, "He *will* come again." Then she disappeared behind a large rock and left the man standing there alone.

He sailed back to Star Island and his hotel not quite sure of what he had seen. He described the woman to several Shoalers but found that none knew of her. His curiosity piqued, he determined to revisit the spot the following day. A storm was blowing when he woke the next morning, and the fishermen on Star tried to convince him not to go, but he was resolved.

After a rough crossing, he pulled his boat into a cove and headed for the cliffs. As the waves crashed and rolled about him, he clambered over the slippery rocks and finally reached the desolate, windswept cliff where he had seen the young woman. There was no sign of her, but through the wind and the rain he heard her sad voice repeating "He will come again," and then the sound of low laughter.

The man returned day after day, and he would see her standing in the same spot, sometimes right next to him. As time passed he believed he could hear her words ringing in his head rather than his ears. Her approach would always be silent, and he observed that the seashells never crunched under her feet. He also noted that even in the gustiest breezes, her hair never stirred from her forehead or shoulders.

The man recalled the last time he saw the ghost-bride. It

was just twilight and a strange sense of peace pervaded the air. He stood on the cliff and waited for the woman to appear, which she did. This time, however, she looked unusually human. There was color in her cheeks, and her cold, empty eyes had grown soft and warm. The man was startled and frightened by this change, and he fell to his knees, swearing never to visit the spot again. It was a promise that he kept.

But what of the pirate bride? In her history, *Among the Isles of Shoals*, Celia Thaxter wonders, "[i]s it she . . . who laments like a Banshee before the tempests, wailing through the gorges at Appledore . . . ?" Thaxter speaks of this apparition frightening picnickers on Duck Island, appearing sometimes as a young girl and at other times "older than the Sphinx in the desert."

The Isles of Shoals today are uninhabited except for some private summer homes. A marine laboratory and a religious conference center, used primarily in the warmer months, are the only scraps of civilization left on Appledore. So, one can imagine, if the pirate bride is still there, she has the whole island to herself now. She may yet be wandering Appledore's cliffs in the snow and the sleet and the gentle summer rain, with her face cast toward the sea and those insistent words on her lips: "He *will* come again."

5

Pirate Ghosts and Haunted Caves

T he islands of Casco Bay stretch from South Portland to the mouth of the Kennebec River. Sometimes referred to as "the Calendar Islands" because it is fancied that there are 365 of them (there are, in fact, only 200 or so), these dots of greenery on the blue waters of the bay are rich in lore and legend. Some of these legends are heroic in theme, some humorous, and some even go so far as to be factual. Others have been tainted with the blood of murder and piracy, and certainly one of the islands best known for the latter is Jewell.

In its earlier years of settlement, the island seems to have attracted many rogues and scoundrels. George Jewell was a hard-drinking sailor who bought the island from the Indians in 1637 in exchange for some gunpowder, a bottle of rum, and a few fishhooks. Basically a squatter, he left little but his name to the island when he drowned in Boston Harbor after a night of revelry. Owing to its numerous hidden coves and to the fact that it is one of the first islands you hail when approaching Portland Harbor from the sea, Jewell has been popular throughout its history as a haven for pirates and smugglers. The most famous of these is none other than Captain Kidd (1645?–1701).

According to various legends, Kidd was cruising near Long Island when a suspicious-looking sail on the horizon caused him to flee around the peninsula of Cape Cod. As he neared the Isles of Shoals, he spied yet another vessel that made him wary, so he continued north to Casco Bay. Looking for a spot to hide his stolen gold and jewels in case he was captured, he picked Jewell Island. Loading all his loot in either a chest or a copper kettle (the legends differ), he rowed ashore to Jewell with his crew of pirates and selected a cove in the southern half of the island. After burying the treasure, Kidd supposedly had his men place a heavy, flat rock over the spot. The pirate leader then etched a compass on the rock with the north indicator pointing south.

As with most pirate legends, this one refers to a treasure map hidden somewhere, supposedly drawn by Kidd and given by him, on his deathbed, to a black servant. The map eventually fell into the hands of a man from St. John, New Brunswick, who came to Casco Bay in the 1860s in search of Kidd's treasure. This man hooked up with a nefarious character who lived on Jewell, named Captain Chase, and solicited his help in finding the treasure. He would cut Chase in on the treasure if the old smuggler would help by supplying the tools and a compass. Chase agreed, and the next thing people knew, the man from St. John was nowhere to be seen and Captain Chase was packing his bags for a little vacation. When questioned about what had happened, old Chase said that the search had been unsuccessful and the St. John man had just left the island. Some curious souls began to wonder, however, and decided to explore the southern part of the island. There, near a little cove, they found a deep, freshly dug hole. In the muddy bottom was the imprint of a chest. It was believed that the St. John man and Chase had found the treasure, split it up, and parted ways. Chase went on to become the wealthiest man on the island and retired quite comfortably.

In this tale fact and fiction tend to blend a bit. First, there is little or no evidence to suggest that Kidd was ever actually in Maine, although avowals of at least his treasure being here exist in documents dating from Revolutionary War days. Also, the story of the treasure map being bequeathed from a deathbed seems shaky, since, as author Dorothy Simpson points out in her book, *The Maine Islands in Story and Legend*, Kidd met his death by hanging.

But there *was* a Captain Chase who lived on Jewell in the mid-1800s, and he was known to have been a pirate and a smuggler and possibly a murderer. He and another pirate named Keif were supposed to have lured ships to the rocky shores of Cliff Island with lanterns. When the ships were wrecked on the sharp rocks, Chase and Keif would kill any poor sailors who hadn't already drowned and then loot the vessels. Chase was also known to have been a go-between for rum smugglers. In his unusual fortresslike stone house, which had narrow portholes for windows, Chase was supposed to have kept stockpiles of the liquor hidden in secret compartments under the floors. He bought the rum from the merchant ships and sold it to the Casco Bay islanders at a discount rate that reaped a profit for him but cheated the government out of its excise tax.

But legends often have some vestige of truth to them, and shortly after Chase's death in the late 1800s, a hunter or a berry picker (again, the stories differ) happened upon a skeleton wedged in a rocky crevice not far from the site of the treasure hole. Decayed beyond physical recognition, there yet remained on the body one distinguishable item—a silver ring that many of the elder islanders said had been worn by the St. John man. It was quickly rumored that the wicked Chase had murdered the man after they had together unearthed Kidd's treasure.

It wasn't long before eerie lights and strange sounds after dark were reported from this end of the island. One islander recounted that, while walking near the treasure site one night, he saw two ghostly figures digging away at something in the bluish glow of a mysterious light. Then the islander heard a scream and a series of groans, and at this point didn't stay around to hear more. From then on, the island was believed to be haunted.

Other stories of murder and piracy are associated with Jewell. A pirate vessel from Bermuda was said to have cruised through Casco Bay in the mid 1800s and struck a rock known as the Brown Cow. As the ship went down, the crew managed to rescue not only themselves but a chest of gold, which they buried on Jewell near what was called Punch Bowl Cove. Old Captain Chase enters the scene again as, years later, he was supposed to have entertained these pirates on their return to Jewell to unearth their treasure. Chase claimed to have found the square hole near Punch Bowl Cove in which the gold had been hidden.

The female pirate Ann Bonney was reputed to have visited Jewell with the intention of burying some treasure there. She had seven members of her crew row her to the island, watched as they buried the gold, and then calmly shot every one of them. In the early 1960s, seven graves with small, unlettered markers were discovered on the island, and some speculated that these were the resting places of the unfortunate sailors who had trusted the murderous pirate Bonney. She met her own fate hanging from the end of a British frigate's yardarm.

More numerous than mysterious gravestones on Jewell have been the "claim markers" left by the many treasure hunters who have combed the island with everything from divining rods to metal detectors looking for the pot of gold that in all likelihood does not exist. At least one person has found something while exploring Jewell's many caverns and grottoes—it wasn't buried treasure, however. What Margaret Newlin of Bangor discovered had nothing to do with pirates, but with the ghosts of men who lived and worked on Jewell Island almost fifty years ago.

During World War II, Jewell was one of the many spots in the bay fortified and garrisoned by the army. Numerous gun batteries with labyrinthine underground caves can be found there to this day. Years after the war, Margaret Newlin's father worked in Casco Bay as a nautical compass adjuster. She used to accompany him during the summers as he made his rounds of the various islands, Jewell being one of them.

Margaret remembers a family visit to the island back in 1977 when she was fifteen years old. Her mother chose to sunbathe on the beach while young Margaret set off to explore the numerous trails that crisscrossed the island's surface.

"It was a beautiful day in the middle of summer," recalls Margaret. "I knew the trails out there pretty well and remember going beyond the observation tower that day, down a dirt road toward the southern end of the island. I came to a tunnel that led out of a big mound next to an old gunnery platform. As I got closer to the opening of the tunnel, I suddenly heard voices coming from inside. I thought there were other explorers there, so I called out 'Hello,' but no one answered. I was curious and got closer—I must have been ten or twelve feet away from the entrance—and then I saw these three men in olive-drab uniforms walking away from the tunnel. They wore helmets or hard hats and I remember vividly that one was wearing wire-rimmed glasses. They looked to be in their thirties or forties. I stood there frozen, and they walked toward me but didn't seem to notice I was there. They seemed content, very casual, and were just talking amongst themselves. I saw one of them pass something to the other, and then they just disappeared."

Margaret ran all the way back to her mother and reported what she had seen, but her mother did not believe her. After that, Margaret kept it to herself for many years, but now says that her family has come to believe her story about the strange incident.

What did Margaret Newlin see that day? The uniforms and the location would indicate that they were the spirits of army personnel stationed on Jewell during the war. Some five hundred men had served there, guarding Casco Bay and spending many tedious days and nights in the cavernous tunnels that housed radio rooms, planning rooms, shell rooms, and powder magazines. Trapped here, perhaps, in some endless routine, the ghosts may continue to walk out of this tunnel, day after day, as they had done in life. It is also possible that they enjoyed their duty here and are reluctant to leave.

If the various legends of Jewell are to be believed, these military phantoms have plenty of company from the likes of Captain Chase and many others who have sunk a surreptitious spade into the island's surface.

Haunted
Houses

6

The Lingering Soul of Father Moriarty

F ather Thomas H. Moriarty arrived in the town of Brewer in 1926 to establish the parish of St. Joseph's. Moriarty was a big, rugged, ruddy-faced fellow—imposing and as Irish as they come. Some residents of Brewer recall how he had a way of riveting you with his eye "like he was going to tear you apart." A former hammer-thrower at Boston College, Moriarty seemed just the man the diocese wanted to shoulder the responsibility of pastoring a new church in this central Maine town. Not only did he roll up his sleeves to take on his assigned post, but he even, on one occasion, had to roll up those same sleeves to defend himself and his church from a band of KKK members who gathered threateningly outside his door one evening.

Yet Father Moriarty's stronger weapons seemed to have

been his gifts for Irish wit and understatement that flourished beneath the gruffness of his exterior. When criticized once by a colleague for being a bit too rough on his parishioners during a sermon, Moriarty replied that he wasn't being hard on them—he was simply "stressing the point." Some who knew him confessed to being frightened of him; those who truly knew him, however, understood that he was actually a very caring, kind, and humble man.

Father Moriarty served the parish of St. Joseph's for over forty years, living across the street from the church in the rectory, which stood at the corner of Holyoke and North Main streets. When his health declined during the early sixties and he was unable to perform all of his duties as pastor, he stayed on at St. Joseph's as "pastor emeritus." In April of 1969, Father Moriarty died, and his funeral service was held at the church he had served so well for so long. Barely forty-eight hours after his death, while his body lay in state in a funeral parlor in Bangor, Father Moriarty's spirit was still at work in the parish rectory.

Father Richard Rice was the assistant pastor at St. Joseph's under Father Moriarty, and he was still serving at the parish when the elder priest died. Father Rice had been newly ordained when he came to Brewer in 1960, and he had developed what he refers to as a "grandfather-grandson relationship" with Moriarty. Two days before the late pastor's funeral, Father Rice recalls being at the rectory in the afternoon doing some work. The only other person in the house was a pastor who had been assigned to serve in Father Moriarty's place. This priest had decided to take a nap while Father Rice was working and was in his room asleep with the door closed. Opposite this room at the top of the stairs was the parish office with a guest bedroom off of it. Below this, on the first floor, was a sitting room in which Father Rice was working.

"It was about one in the afternoon," recalls Father Rice, "when I heard some footsteps on the floor above me. It sounded to me like pacing back and forth, such as a priest does when saying his breviary, or daily office. The footsteps continued for twenty minutes or half an hour, and I thought that the pastor had woken from his nap and was saying his prayers. I went to the bottom of the stairs and looked up, but saw that his door was still closed. I checked out the window and saw that the custodian was working outside the church, so I knew that it couldn't be he who was making the noise. Then I thought it might have been a visiting priest in town for Father Moriarty's funeral service, so I went upstairs to greet him. When I got to the bedroom where the noise was coming from, though, I found it empty."

At this point, Father Rice had to go over to the church to hear confessions and celebrate the vigil Mass. At dinner time, however, he questioned the new pastor about the pacing he had heard that afternoon.

"Oh," replied the new pastor casually, "that was Father Moriarty."

Father Rice began to laugh, but the pastor became serious and explained that what the young priest may have heard was really a sign from God that Father Moriarty was all right.

"If Father Moriarty wanted to see this house again—the house in which he lived all these years—well, why not?" said the pastor.

This gave the young Father Rice something to think about over the ensuing weeks, as more was heard from the spirit of Father Moriarty: drawers opened and closed by themselves, and again footsteps sounded in the bedroom of the church's founder. The strange happenings continued over the next several years. Then in 1976 a new rectory was built a few blocks away and the old place was sold to Dr. John H. Hart, a practicing chiropractor, and his family.

"I don't believe in these things," Dr. Hart said when he was informed by the pastor of St. Joseph's that along with the old rectory he had also "bought a ghost." Yet after living there for four years, Dr. Hart confesses that things had occurred for which he just had no explanation.

Hart and his wife also heard the sound of footsteps coming from the bedroom at the head of the stairs, yet the doctor reasoned that since it was an old house with steam heat, the banging of the pipes was probably responsible for the noise. Hart's wife heard voices throughout the house, but again the doctor was skeptical, believing that they might have come from the radio of a passing car, as the house was situated at a major intersection. But then there was the issue of the shattered plate.

"It was one of those plates that was guaranteed to be unbreakable," says Dr. Hart. "My wife had left it on the pantry shelf with some cookies on it before we went to bed one night. When we came down the next morning, the cookies were still there on the plate, and the plate was still on the shelf, but it was shattered. Nothing had fallen on it—it was just in a million pieces."

Dr. Hart believed that, maybe, if nicked just right, the plate might have been broken by him or his wife without their noticing it; he admits, however, that "it was a tough one to try and explain." Shattered plates, though, seem inconsequential in the face of moving objects, such as Dr. Hart and some of his overnight guests experienced one night.

"I had an old frat brother of mine visiting me with his wife and their two-year-old child," Dr. Hart recalls. "They had brought their baby's crib with them, and the three were sleeping in the room at the head of the stairs. About two in the morning, we heard the baby crying. My buddy and his wife also were awakened, and they found that neither their baby nor the crib was in the room anymore. Now, there was a long hallway outside the bedroom and all the lights were out. Suddenly the lights went on, and we saw the baby in the crib at the end of the hallway. There was no way a two-year-old child could have moved that crib out of the room and down that hallway and not woken us up—let alone done it by himself. He wasn't even out of the crib. I simply have no idea how it happened."

Dr. Hart's wife, Cathy, was more convinced than her husband that there must have been someone or something else living in the old rectory with them. The noises she heard, she was certain, were not banging pipes but deliberate footsteps going up the stairs and pacing back and forth in the bedroom. The voices she heard drifting through the house were male voices, and she heard them at all times during the year, not just in the summertime when the windows by the intersection were open On one occasion, she heard water running forcefully in the house somewhere, as if someone were taking a shower. She followed the sound throughout the house, yet everywhere she went, she heard it somewhere else, as if the sound were fleeing from her. These phenomena occurred right up until the Harts moved out of the rectory in 1980.

The old St. Joseph's rectory has since become a boarding house known as the Mayor's Inn Its owner states that although she herself has not had any odd experiences there, her caretaker has told her that sometimes lights have suddenly and inexplicably gone on in the place at all hours.

If you were to ask Father Richard Rice how this could be, he would answer you as calmly as his pastor had at St. Joseph's the day he first heard the footsteps in the bedroom. "There are a lot of things we don't know," says Father Rice "The Lord allows for whatever He wishes. He is the author of us all. I believe these noises and sounds are sometimes a sign from the Lord for a need for prayer for one who has died, a very strong sign that prayers would be in order for the eternal repose of this man of God, Father Moriarty. I believe that this could also be a sign from God that all is well with Father Moriarty and that his spirit still dwells with us."

That this "spirit" Father Rice refers to may indeed still be with us is borne out by one last unusual event. Not long ago, a new family moved into Brewer. The wife was outside in her yard washing the windows of her new home when she noticed a priest walking across the lawn to greet her. He introduced himself and then asked whether she and her family were Catholic.

"Yes," she replied. "Yes, we are."

"Then why," thundered the priest, "haven't I seen you down at church?"

The woman apologized, saying that with all the chaos of moving in she hadn't had the time. The priest made her promise to be there with her family the following Sunday and went on his way. When the woman told her neighbor about the incident, the neighbor was a bit surprised. It didn't sound like the behavior of the current pastor at St. Joseph's.

"What was the priest's name?" asked the neighbor.

"Father Moriarty."

7

The Woman in the Shawl

The James Forder House—a three-story, mid-eighteenth-century, gray-clapboard affair—sits proudly and innocently enough on a high rise overlooking the Fore River in what is present-day Westbrook, formerly known as Stroudwater. Built in 1734, the house has been passed along through relatively few owners, considering its age. By the time of our story, an apartment had been created from some second floor rooms that face the river. It was in December of 1985 that John Wilson, a history student at the University of Southern Maine, rented the apartment from the owners of the house, who lived downstairs. Wilson's tenure in the apartment would be an extremely short one—barely a week in fact.

"You can't sleep with your eyes wide open and your heart beating a hundred and twenty times a minute," Wilson explained. Here is the reason.

Mary Wilson, John's sister, was the first to sense that there was something strange about the apartment, especially at a certain window near a corner that faced the water. On a midwinter afternoon, as John was moving in, Mary was standing in his bedroom while he was busy unloading some of his things from the car. She stepped over to the window to look at the river when she suddenly felt enveloped by a strange chill. Then she had what she later described as a vision.

She saw a woman with long brunette hair and her shoulders wrapped in a shawl. The woman was standing on the banks of the river watching a man in a rowboat. With her were two small children in knickers who were also watching the rower in the boat. Just as suddenly as this spectacle appeared, it vanished. She was, naturally, disturbed by what she had seen but decided not to mention it to her brother. As it turned out, she didn't have to, for the woman by the river was destined to return.

Several days later, after John had settled into his new apartment, he was awakened about 4:30 one morning by a stifling heat. He got out of bed to open the window a crack—the same window from which his sister had seen the uncanny party at the shore. He fell back asleep, but woke again just before dawn, this time because the room was cold. As he tossed and turned beneath the covers, he happened to open his eyes and look down at the end of his bed, which was close to the window. Suddenly, in the gray half-light of the winter dawn, he saw a woman standing in his room in front of the window. It was a solid image John saw, not a translucent figure. The woman wore an old-fashioned dress and a bone-colored shawl. A long trail of brunette hair hung at her back and curls of it peeked out from beneath the end of her wrap. The woman's right hand was at her breast and her left hand held the folds of the shawl together. She was simply standing at the window with what John has described as a "thoughtful" look on her face.

The young student was terrified. He stayed perfectly still, and his first thought was that someone had broken into his apartment. Then, as his fear grew, he closed his eyes with the empty hope that whatever or whoever it was would just go away. When he reopened his eyes, the woman was still there, only this time standing a little closer to the window. John then decided to do something. Speaking to the figure, he said slowly and cautiously, "Please . . . please, don't hurt me."

When he said this, the woman turned toward him as if only just recognizing that he was there. "Then she just vanished," says John. "I sat up in bed and looked around, but there was nothing or nobody there."

John was horribly shaken by the incident, and the first person he reported it to was his sister. It was then that Mary related to him the vision she had had. Mary was an artist, and as John told her the details of the disquieting event, she drew a picture of the woman she had seen by the river. John immediately recognized her, right down to the curls below the shawl. John attempted to spend another couple of nights in his new apartment but found that he couldn't sleep with the memory of the strange woman at the window still in his mind. He had an interest in the occult and believed that the appearance of ghosts was "in the realm of possibility," but contact of this sort, in his own bedroom, was just too much for the young man to bear. Two days afterward, he moved out of the apartment and in with his sister. He has never wanted to go back to the Forder House again.

The present owner of the house states that neither she nor any member of her family has had any experiences akin to those of the Wilson's at the house. She recalled, however, that a previous tenant, Jean Paul Poulain, was living in the apartment in 1983 and did have some encounters very much like John and Mary Wilson's. Poulain says that he would often hear strange knockings and noises coming from the downstairs.

"They were very loud and distinct. Bumps and knocks, and chains dragging across the floor. The people who lived there before me said they used to hear things down in the kitchen but thought it might be rodents," says Poulain. It was, as coincidence would have it, in the winter that Poulain says he had his one and only visual experience with the phantom of the Forder House.

"It was at night. I was crossing through the main part of the house downstairs when suddenly I got the strange sensation that something or someone was there. It was a cold, chilling feeling, like someone had opened the door of a refrigerator in front of me. Then I saw a woman in nineteenth-century clothing sitting on a couch before the fireplace. She was milky and transparent, but I could easily see details like her hair, which was long and flowing."

The figure was almost floating there, and Poulain stopped dead in his steps when he saw it. He spoke to it, asking if he could do anything to help. "After I said this, she just went away. I never saw her again, but the sounds of the chains continued, off and on, during the whole time I was living there."

Who is this woman with the long, flowing hair and the shawl occupying the house and grounds of the Forder House? It is difficult to say. As we have seen in other similar accounts, a house or an area may become haunted if there is some human tragedy associated with the place. This tragedy need not be as spectacular or horrible as a murder or suicide, but can be as simply saddening as a death in the family. This may be the case at the James Forder House, as history tells us that a family by the name of Lobdell lived there in the early 1800s. Isaac Lobdell, Jr., a sea captain, and his wife, Mary, lived in the Forder House with Isaac Sr. and their nine children. The last of these were twins born in October 1799. One twin, Edward Gray, died after only three days; his brother Charles survived almost two years, dying in August 1801. Their sad little gravestone in the family plot reads:

> Sleep on sweet Babes from Sorrow Free
> Thy parents soon will come to thee . .

Could it be that the ghost of Mary Lobdell still lingers in the house, entrapped by the sadness of her infant sons' deaths?

Does she stand guard by the window of the second floor or by the banks of the Fore River, up which she and her family first sailed in 1795, in silent and passive mourning? Does she still wait, for some inexplicable reason, to go join her twin sons and the rest of the Lobdells? We cannot truly say. The woman in the shawl at the Forder House will speak to no one and only seems to watch and wait, and fade before she can tell us why she waits.

8

The Protective Child

Oftentimes, spirits can be quite protective of the spaces they occupy and even of the persons sharing that space with them. Such was the case at a two-hundred-year-old house in Norway, Maine.

Joe and Brenda, the young couple that lived in the house, started to have strange experiences there soon after their first child was born. Their child's room was at the top of the stairs. On several occasions, when they heard Nicky crying and went in to check on him, they were startled to find the baby sitting on the floor outside the crib. Since Nicky was less than a year old, Joe and Brenda were sure there was no way he could have gotten out of the crib by himself. Other strange happenings took place in the room when the weather was rainy or windy. Even when Brenda was sure she had left the windows in the room open, upon going to close them against the storm she would find them already shut.

On one occasion, the baby's grandmother, Maureen, was babysitting while the couple was out for the evening. When Maureen heard the baby suddenly begin to cry, she started up the stairs. Before she had reached the second floor, she was shocked to see the family's cat come flying through the air as if it had been hurled out of the room. She hurried up the stairs and, once more, found the child out of his crib, unharmed, sitting on the floor.

Convinced now that something very strange was going on in their home, Brenda and Joe had a psychic visit them. The psychic toured the house, concentrating his attention on the child's room. Through telepathy, the psychic learned that a three-year-old child had suffocated in the house, in the very room that was now Nicky's nursery. The boy had been fond of a pet cat, and when the unfortunate parents had found their son dead, the cat was asleep next to him in the bed.

The psychic went on to learn that the spirit of the three-year-old was now occupying the room and protecting Joe and Brenda's baby. When it rained, he closed the windows; if the cat came too close to the crib, he forced it out of the room. Indeed, after the cat had been flung through the doorway as Maureen witnessed, it would never enter the room again. The psychic explained that the cat had probably seen the ghost of the child walking around the crib and was simply frightened of the apparition.

The psychic asked Joe and Brenda if they wanted him to persuade the little ghost to leave the house. They thought about this, but declined. It had never actually harmed the baby, and it may have even prevented Nicky from hurting himself on those occasions when it removed him from the crib. They decided that they were even pleased, in a way, to have another watchful eye standing guard over their baby.

Eventually Joe and Brenda moved out of the house in Norway and went to Massachusetts. As far as is known, the ghost-child never haunted the room again.

AUTHOR'S NOTE: In this account, all names of participants have been changed to protect their identities.

9

The Ghost in
the Cellar

W illiam E. Gould didn't have much opportunity to enjoy his lavish new brick residence on Portland's fashionable State Street. He built the rambling Victorian structure in 1884, and in 1886 he was sent to jail for embezzling $27,000 from the First National Bank, where he worked as a cashier. He spent five years in the state penitentiary, after which he returned to humbler quarters in the city.

His fine home on State Street came into the hands of one James H. McMullen, who lived there until 1920. The Gould house stood vacant for one year after this, until a group of physicians purchased it for an office building. It remained so until the early 1970s, when the owners created a few apartments in the building, and gradually it became strictly an apartment house.

Checkered linoleum floors and pebbled-glass doors in the hallway, dating from the physicians' days, still exist side-by-side with the time-blackened mahogany scrollwork and other High Victorian features of Gould's time. One still gets a very real sense of the past there just by standing in the foyer and looking up at the high ceilings and ornate molding. For some, that sense of the past has been a bit too strong.

"Lots of people have moved in and out of here," says Sunshyne Raffa, one resident of the building. "Many have been driven out. There has been trouble in this place; I can feel that."

Sunshyne moved into the Gould house in 1987. She is psychic and says she has sensed a strong energy in the house, particularly in the basement.

"I have sensed rituals going on down there," she says. "Indian ceremonies. I believe that this was once an Indian graveyard, and perhaps when a house was built here, a few of the bodies were not exhumed."

Sunshyne says that "another dimension sometimes slides through into this one," and that is when spirits may be encountered at the Gould house. Such an incident took place in the laundry room one day.

"I felt apprehensive before going down there that day," recalls Sunshyne. "I was busy taking my clothes out of the machine when I felt someone tap me on the shoulder. I turned around and there was no one there. I got out of there fast, and when I was in the hallway upstairs I felt a hand again brush by me. I don't go into the laundry room anymore. I don't even like to be in the basement."

Leanne McCormick took one of the basement apartments in the spring of 1988. The apartment is adjacent to the laundry room, and the bedroom is connected to it by a small unused hallway. Her bed was against the wall nearest the hallway.

"One night, while I was asleep I heard someone walking around the room," she recalls. "It was a pacing sound. At first, I thought it might be my cat, but then I noticed that the cat was there in bed with me. That's when I got scared. I stayed still, listening to it for a while, and then I finally sat up. When I did, the moving stopped."

Still frightened, Leanne felt her bed become "burning hot." She got up quickly and then noticed that the room itself was extremely cold. When she moved toward the bed again, she could still feel the heat. She and her upstairs neighbor, Sunshyne, had spoken before about paranormal activity, and she had been advised to tell a spirit to "go into the light" if it was bothering her.

"I just told it to head into the light," says Leanne, "and I finally got back to sleep."

Leanne continued to have trouble sleeping in this part of her room until she moved her bed into another corner. "After that," she says "the trouble in my room stopped."

But there were other incidents that pointed to a haunting in Leanne's apartment. She would hear movements in her closet at night. Through a nail hole in the wall facing the unused hallway, she would sometimes see a light when she knew no light had been left on there.

"The door from the laundry room to that hallway was always locked from my side. I was the only one who could have left a light on in there, and I knew I hadn't."

While lying in bed, she would sometimes hear glasses, plates, and pans being moved about in her kitchen. She inspected the cupboards for mice and saw no sign of them. In one corner of her living room she kept a chair that would "give you a creepy feeling to sit in."

"It was always cold in that corner, too. My cat would go wild on that chair. It would jump at it and attack it, as if there were someone sitting there."

Leanne had a roommate for a brief time, who encountered the spirit while she was taking a bath one morning. Leanne was at work, the bathroom door was closed, and the apartment was empty. Suddenly, the roommate heard and saw the door-knob move back and forth slowly, as if someone were trying to get in. Frightened, she got out of her bath to see if it might be Leanne, but found no one there.

Leanne believed that there was something in her apartment looking for a way out, trying to find its freedom, searching for a way into another world. Some of her neighbors in the building, who have also had odd experiences there, believe there could be restless spirits looking for their doctors, who once practiced in the building.

Sunshyne, despite her fear of the basement, says she feels "protected" because of her psychic abilities. She has noted how, simultaneously, pets in the building will act strangely, and she maintains that animals can sense spiritual activity and are even capable of seeing ghosts when humans cannot. "Animals, and sometimes small children, have not been told that there are no such things as ghosts," she says. "They don't have that prejudice, that disbelief, and so they can witness these things."

A fireplace in Sunshyne's apartment features a hideous-looking demon cast into the metal fireback. She has noticed how her cat "freaks out" when it is near the fireplace. She said that when she kept her bed by the fireplace she always had restless nights.

"I would often dream that I fell out of bed and into the fireplace," she recalls. Finally, she moved her bed to another part of the room just to get a peaceful night's sleep.

The spirit (or spirits?) in the Gould house could be just about anyone, it seems. Perhaps, as Sunshyne Raffa says, it is the restless phantom of a buried Indian; perhaps it is a disgruntled patient, coming back to plague a doctor who is no longer there; or perhaps it is Gould himself, attempting to enjoy, at last, the splendor of his home on State Street—a pleasure he robbed himself of while here on earth.

10

Get Out!

Susan Small was already familiar with the oddities of the old house at the end of the road in Orrington when she moved there in September 1977. She and her friend Anne Stuart had often visited the place to spend time with their boyfriends, who had lived in the house since 1976. The messages written on the walls in certain rooms made it plain enough to all of them that they were not welcome there. Phrases such as "get out," "leave me alone," and "this is the house of madness" proclaimed that there had been a troubled soul here once. Yet as Anne and Susan and others were to find out, that troubled soul still lingered in the house, emphasizing its presence, making itself known, insisting upon its solitude.

Susan and Anne were in the kitchen helping to clean the place the first week their boyfriends moved in. They thought the words written in pencil in an unsteady hand at different levels on the walls were odd, but they had heard that an old invalid woman had lived in the house for years and so excused the defacements. Their boyfriends had helped them move the stove so they could clean and paint behind it; then the two men left on an errand. Shortly after this, while Susan and Anne vere busy cleaning in another part of the room, the stove's timer suddenly went off. It jarred the two women, and they quickly shut it off. Certainly, moving the old stove might have jolted a wire or tripped the switch, but there was something else wrong; both women began to sense a "weird feeling" in the house, as if they were not alone there. They decided to wait outside for their boyfriends to return. When they tried to open the kitchen door, however, they found it mysteriously locked—from the inside.

This was merely their first introduction to the spirit of the house. After they had painted all of the walls in the kitchen and, especially, in the front room and in one particular upstairs bedroom, they found that they would have to do so again and again. "I'm crazy," "you're crazy," and the hauntingly imperative "get out" would reappear on the walls overnight or perhaps while they were all away during the day. These words, however, had not bled through the new paint; they were new words written always in pencil, in spots where they had not been before In time, Susan and Anne just cleaned the words off the wall with soap and water, knowing that the hostile phrases would return to taunt them again. In perhaps the most bizarre instance, Anne saw "get out" written on a window in what she was later told by an authority on the paranormal was ectoplasm. At other times, Susan came home to find the substance running down the walls in the kitchen.

"It was strange stuff," she said. "You'd rub it between your fingers and it would go away. It was sticky and slimy, though, and it seemed to leak from the walls."

The spirit of the house chose other ways to leave its mark on the walls. A new roommate, Janet, had a strange experience while she was painting the area near the ceiling in one room. She took a break from her work, and when she returned to her chore, she found a handprint in the fresh paint. She was certain it was not hers, and no one else had entered the room. When she pointed this out to her housemates, one of the men uneasily related how he had painted the floor in that room when he first moved in and had discovered a footprint in the paint. No one had entered the freshly painted room.

The night hours seemed to be when the spirit was most active. Susan recalls being awakened from her sleep by the sound of water slowly spilling onto the floor, as if someone were pouring it from a pitcher. She turned on her light and inspected the whole floor but found it dry. Anne and her boyfriend slept in a front upstairs bedroom where mysterious handwriting frequently appeared. One night she woke feeling that there was someone else in the room with them. She looked over at the window and saw the pale, white, glowing outline of a figure leaning out of the window. She closed her eyes, and when she opened them again, the light was gone. Janet sometimes woke in the mornings to find that all the extension cords in her bedroom had been pulled apart. One particular evening, she felt a strange pressure on her chest pushing her down into the bed. Fearfully, she told it to go away and it stopped.

Susan says that she would never stay in the house by herself. In fact, not many tenants ever did. On one occasion when Anne happened to be there alone, she was taking a bath in the downstairs bathroom. Just off the bathroom was a room with a woodstove. Anne recalls that there were just a few low embers in the stove's firebox when she went to take her bath. After she was done, she came out to see that the stove was ablaze with fresh logs. She later queried her housemates to see if anyone had come home and stoked the stove, but no one had been in the house at the time.

These and other incidents continued the whole time Susan and Anne and their friends lived in the house. Little items on tables and in cupboards would be moved; pictures on walls would be pushed askew; windows that were shut would be found open; Susan came home once to find a full kettle of water on the stove boiling away furiously when no one had been in the house all day long. Anne's dog would not go near parts of the house, and she sometimes found it growling at a wall or window for no apparent reason; at other times she found the dog trembling and whimpering at nothing at all.

"Eventually, there was a lot of denial going on with all of

us," admits Susan. "We just didn't want to deal with it. We'd joke about it sometimes, but when slime is oozing through the walls, you find it hard to ignore."

The present owners of the house in Orrington report that they have never had any experiences such as the ones Anne and Susan witnessed. Perhaps the lingering spirit had its say and then disappeared. Who this spirit was is anyone's guess. Both Susan and Anne believe it was an old woman who used to live there and who was rumored to have been insane. Sequestered there for years in the house at the end of the road, the woman's spirit perhaps took umbrage at the new tenants and tried its best to get them to leave. Leave they did, after a long, troubled year in residence with a ghost.

11

The Footless Ghost of Benton Falls

A child's toy—a simple musical mechanism that started without cause and ended without explanation: the haunting melody of an unlocatable music box that floated through the many rooms of the old Buzzel house in Benton Falls was just one of the strange phenomena that the McComb family experienced after they purchased the house in the autumn of 1963. The McCombs were nothing out of the ordinary, except perhaps by virtue of number—six sons and a daughter—and they had no reason to believe that the house they had just bought was any more exceptional. That is, until things started to happen.

It was the summer of 1964 and the family's eldest son, Michael, came home to find the house empty. He had settled down to read in the living room while awaiting the arrival of his parents or one of his siblings when Butch, the family dog, began to growl and bark at the bottom of the stairs. Michael wondered what had frightened the dog. Suddenly he heard footsteps on the second floor. The steps were slow and clear and definite. As the dog pawed at the steps and the hair on its back began to rise, Michael called up to the second floor, but the only response he got was the steady thump of footsteps. Now as frightened as Butch, he quickly left the house. When he told his family of it later, they wouldn't believe him, thinking he was joking—that is, until the following Christmas.

It was almost midnight when Jean, then ten years old, woke to the sounds of heavy breathing. Then she heard footsteps, which began in the hallway and ended in the corner of her room. There was a small Christmas tree in that corner and Jean could hear the presents below the tree being picked up and "pawed over."

The following Christmas, one of the McComb sons, Robert, was home on leave from the Marine Corps. That night he was sleeping in a third-floor bedroom just above Jean's. The stairs from the second floor ended directly across the hall from his bedroom door. In the middle of the night, Robert heard footsteps coming up the stairs. Hearing a stair squeak, he sat up and looked out into the darkness of the hall, where a window at the top of the stairs let in the meager light of the winter evening. Robert saw a shadow pass by the window and then by his bedroom door. The footsteps continued down the hall to a small, empty bedroom. Robert was so frightened that he ran into the next room and jumped into bed with his brother Frank.

On another occasion, Doug McComb was lying in his bed on the second floor around 7:30 a.m. The headboard of his bed was just inside the door, and if he leaned out of bed a little, he had a clear view of the hallway and the staircase. That morning, young Doug heard footsteps on the stairs slowly making their way up to the second floor. Cautiously, he leaned over to have a look and was surprised to see no one there. The disembodied footsteps paused at the second-floor landing and then continued on up to the third floor.

Similar occurrences continued to haunt the place, yet John McComb, the father, still remained skeptical about his home being anything more than a normal house—until one bright autumn day when he heard glass breaking throughout the house. After searching all the rooms and finding no broken glass anywhere, Mr. McComb began to wonder.

The McCombs were not the only people who were witness to ghostly and uncanny happenings at the Buzzel house. A young cousin was visiting one day and entered Jean's bedroom. Suddenly she heard a wicker chair in the corner creak as if someone were rising from it, together with an exasperated sigh. Then she heard the footsteps, this time with one foot dragging, cross slowly before her.

In September of 1970, the McCombs made a discovery that they believed might be the clue to the curious and haunting events in their house. While tearing out an old partition, they found a small mummified foot hidden in the wall. They sent it to a Boston laboratory, where it was identified as a child's foot that had been amputated sometime in the early 1900s. Research into the house's history disclosed that it had once been owned by a physician. The McCombs believed that this foot was from one of his young patients. In those times, it was not uncommon for people to preserve amputated limbs so they could later be buried together with the bodies. Was the ghostly inhabitant of their home a poor crippled child in search of its lost limb? The McCombs believe so.

After the foot was discovered, the uncanny occurrences at the McComb residence seemed to increase. On that very night, Bill McComb was awakened by the sound of the shutters outside his bedroom window opening. They were then hurled apart and banged loudly against the outside of the house. The shutters had been held in place by two separate sets of eyehook locks, which Bill was certain he had securely fastened before going to bed that night.

The senior McCombs were aural witnesses to another event. The children were all at school and Mr. McComb was asleep in his bedroom. Mrs. McComb, awake and in the same room, heard the sound of a foot and cane tapping loudly on the floor upstairs. The noise was so pronounced that it woke Mr. McComb. This noise, as had many of the other ghostly manifestations, such as the sound of the music box, sounded as if it were coming from Jean's room. The young girl by this time had been sleeping downstairs in the living room most nights because of all the unexplained activity that seemed to center in her room. Perhaps the most telling evidence of this was when some members of the family moved a large trunk in Jean's room. Beneath the trunk, imprinted in the dust, was the image of a bare right foot. The impression didn't match any family member's foot.

The McCombs finally sold the house, and the new owners don't believe in ghosts. Neither did the McCombs, however, until they moved into the Buzzel house. Since there hasn't been any recent supernatural activity there, perhaps the ghost has found what it was looking for and is now at last at peace.

AUTHOR'S NOTE: Members of the McComb family—whose names have been changed in this chapter to preserve their anonymity—were unwilling to talk at length about their experiences at the Buzzel house in Benton Falls. What they did admit was that something happened there that was very real to them all. This account of their experiences was reconstructed primarily from newspaper reports of the time, written just after the family discovered the foot in the the wall.

12

The Chinese Curse of Naples

I n the mid-1800s, the doors of ancient China were opened to the West, and through those doors the traders and investors of another culture poured in quest of the famed wonders and riches of the Orient. Some established peaceful trade, yet others were less than diplomatic. Our story concerns one such man, Charles Hill, of Naples, Maine.

Hill's family was in the tea-trading business and owned property in Tientsin, just south of Peking. He was a wealthy man who also held vast interests in one of China's first railroad systems. Although Britain, France, and the United States had succeeded in establishing lines of trade with the Manchu emperors, the Chinese looked upon the Westerners essentially as barbarians and often cursed them, calling them "fan kuei," or "foreign devil." The resentment of the Chinese went far beyond cultural snobbery, for it was the British and the Americans who were largely responsible for promoting the debilitating addiction to opium among the Chinese. Since the Chinese felt that the West had nothing to offer them in the form of goods, they would accept only hard currency—silver coins or the raw bullion known as sycee—in exchange for their precious tea, silk, and porcelain. In order to get the required silver with which to purchase these export items, U.S. traders dealt in opium, turning the money around quickly and making a handsome profit. In doing so, however, they were also perpetuating the virtual enslavement of hundreds of thousands of Chinese—an enslavement to the "foreign mud" from the poppy fields of Turkey and India.

As the number of addicts in the country reached the millions, the Chinese officials, under an imperial order, forbade the trading of opium, yet the practice continued. On many occasions over the course of the late nineteenth century, Chinese insurgents took matters into their own hands and rebelled against the "foreign devils," forcing many of them to flee the country for their lives. It was just such an occasion that caused Charles Hill to leave Tientsin and make a hasty return to Maine. Before he fled, however, he and some of his companions paid a visit to a local Buddhist temple, which they had heard was famous for its rich statuary and treasures. Boldly and irreverently brandishing their weapons in the midst of the peaceful worshippers, Hill and his men looted the place, carrying off gold, precious jewels, and three huge bronze idols. Returning with these to Maine, Hill erected the statues at his home in Naples, then known as Bellevue Terrace.

The massive idols were a curious sight. Standing over eight feet tall, they depicted warrior Buddhas, replete with armor and helmets, in passive defiance with hands clasped prayerfully together. Situated at the bottom of Bellvue Terrace's main stairway, amidst an already sumptuously decorated late Victorian interior, the idols must have been an imposing spectacle to any guest entering the house. With their cold cheeks shining dully beneath watchful yet threatening Oriental eyes, the statues almost seemed to be waiting, patiently, for revenge.

When they first took the idols, the Hill party noticed how heavy they were. After Hill got them back to Maine, he discovered why—the figures were literally filled with gold and jewels. Hill melted down the gold and sold some of the jewels, reaping a $300,000 profit (quite a sum back then), with which he set about building an addition to his house. It was the last constructive thing that would happen to Bellevue Terrace.

Years later, when the Hill family fortune began to dwindle, Charles Hill made another trip to China in search of more riches. He was even so bold as to revisit the temple he had so blasphemously robbed, only this time he didn't fare as well. The priests there well recalled the desecrater of their temple and when Hill entered the temple grounds, they fell upon him and his party in a murderous frenzy. As the cries of the terrified white men rang out in the quiet of the forest, the priests placed a curse on Hill's property and all who lived there. When the Hill family finally heard of Charles Hill's fate and the curse, they reportedly heaved the idols into Long Lake or buried them somewhere on the premises.

In 1891, the Hills sold Bellevue Terrace to one John S. White and his family. Although Charles Hill's descendents left Maine, they had apparently left one thing behind—the Chinese curse. Thirty years after the Whites bought Bellvue Terrace, the last surviving member of the family, Charles R. White, was found dead floating in the waters off Portland's Eastern Promenade. The medical examiner ruled White's death a suicide. There was a revolver "near the body and withdrawn but slightly from the holster." Two bullets had been discharged from the chamber, one of which had found its way through White's heart; the police conjectured that a reflex action was responsible for the firing of the second bullet.

Public reaction to White's death was one of shock and confusion. White had been a Congressional Medal of Honor winner, a distinction he had received for saving the life of a drowning man not far from where he had met his own mysterious demise. He was a successful local author and a respected citizen of both Portland and Naples, and thus the tragic event left many people wondering and some even recalling the now arcane details of the Hill property curse.

In 1926, Bellevue Terrace was purchased by Mr. and Mr. Charles Sodens. The Sodenses were a wealthy couple who summered in Naples, and Mrs. Sodens set up an antiques shop and tea room at the Hill house, renaming it the Hayloft. The changing of a name could not change the dreadful stigma attached to the property, however. The Sodenses' business failed, they lost a good deal of their money, and finally Mr. Sodens was found dead; he had hanged himself. A year later, his wife died quite suddenly.

The Hill property passed through various owners who tried but failed to keep some type of business going there. In 1950, Mr. and Mrs. Philip Clark, a couple from Connecticut, bought the property sight unseen through a real estate agent. Four months after they moved in, Mrs. Clark had a bad fall and broke her hip. While she recuperated in the hospital, Mr. Clark stayed alone at the house, which the couple had renamed Serenity Hill. On a bitterly cold night in February 1951, Serenity Hill burned to the ground in a fire that claimed the life of Mr. Clark. The property later passed from Mrs. Clark to some of her descendents, who built and operated a nightclub there for some years that had a reputation for being a horribly violent place—so dangerous that the police would only go there in teams to quell disturbances.

In the late seventies, the property was purchased by the Living Waters Fellowship Congregation. The barn, which was the only original building left on the property, is currently a religious meeting house. Perhaps the curse has been eradicated with time. Perhaps. One of the idols did turn up, though, in a dark corner of the Boston Museum of Fine Arts, and was returned to Naples, where it can be seen at the local historical museum.

13

The Haunted Castle

Sylvester B. Beckett was sixty-two years old in 1874, when he built the stone "cottage" that came to be known as "Beckett's Castle" in Cape Elizabeth. By this time, he had already gone to sea and been shipwrecked in the West Indies; had worked on newspapers in Alabama and in Portland; had been admitted to the Cumberland bar; had served on the school committee and the Board of Assessors; had been instrumental in the founding of Portland's Evergreen Cemetery (where he was interred); had published the first Portland Directory and Reference Book; had been voted an honorary member of the Maine Press Association; and had published a book on birds, a guidebook to the White Mountains, and a 336-page lyric poem entitled "Hester, the Bride of the Islands."

It was Beckett's vision in his later years to build a replica of an old English castle on a bluff overlooking Casco Bay. Although the cottage bears little actual resemblance to a castle (outside of the stonework and a thirty-foot-square tower), it came to be known as "the Castle" nonetheless and was the gathering place for many local artists, writers, journalists, and thinkers of Beckett's day. Beckett lived here for eight years, until he died in December of 1882. Yet, had you been able to speak with him, Sylvester Beckett would not have said that he died. He eschewed using that term for what happens to the soul after the body gives up its life

> Life, spirit, soul! they come and go
> But whence or whither who can say?
> A something dwells within, we know,
> And finds expression through the clay . .

> If the soul dieth, if our years
> On earth, of discord, joys and tears,
> Be all of life, then life is vain
> And Heaven's great work imperfect! No

> No! death is but the second birth—
> And man, immortal, oft returns . . .

> Such things are not illusions—nay!
> Nay!—still do man-immortals sway
> In life's affairs! and often blend
> With souls of earth, in sweet commune . . .

> FROM "HESTER, THE BRIDE OF THE ISLANDS: A POEM,"
> BY SYLVESTER B. BECKETT, PORTLAND, BAILEY & NOYES, 1860.

Some persons who have since lived in Beckett's Castle might agree. There is even one documented instance in which someone has spoken with the deceased Beckett. That someone is Alex Tanous, a noted psychic, who, along with journalist Lynne Campbell, visited Beckett's Castle in 1982, one hundred years after Beckett had passed away.

An assignment from The Portland Chronicle to investigate Beckett's Castle put Lynne Campbell in touch with both Alex Tanous and the late Robert Lins, who was living in the house at the time. Lins told Campbell that the place was certainly haunted, and by more than one ghost. He showed her a nail on the kitchen wall just above the stove. He said that he had hung a painting on the nail four times and that four times he found the painting wedged behind the stove with its face reversed. He reported how he had been held in place by "unseen hands" in the living room on one occasion. The door leading from his bedroom to the tower, Lins said, would not stay shut. He tried every means he could think of to keep the door closed and finally, in desperation, nailed it shut.

"As I left the room," he told Campbell, "the nails flew out of the wall, just missing my head."

During one midwinter storm, the front door burst open and a hot wind blew through the house and exited through the back door, which similarly opened with unaccountable force.

After hearing all this from Lins, Campbell decided to bring in the help of an expert. Dr. Alex Tanous is a teacher of parapsychology at the University of Southern Maine, holds several degrees, and has written numerous books on the subject of psychic activity. A psychic himself (*psionic*, he prefers to call it), Tanous has toured the world in search of spirits.

Tanous had simply been told that there had been some unusual activity taking place at Beckett's Castle. He was not briefed with any of the details supplied by Lins. When he toured the house for the first time, he immediately sensed that there were a number of "entities" there.

"I keep hearing motions of people walking," he said as he wandered about the rooms and hallways of the house. "There have been a number of artists here. Some of them have died. I sense they are still painting."

Tanous continued to sense the presence of these "entities" as he made his way upstairs. When he came to Lins's bedroom door, he noted particularly powerful sensations.

"Someone had a confrontation with one of the entities here," he said. "This was very strong. Physical. It was very real."

It was Tanous's eventual conclusion that Sylvester Beckett was still there in the house, together with some other spirits.

He believed that Beckett's spirit, however, was the most dominant.

"This was his corner of the world," said Tanous. "His heaven. Anyone intruding on that is certainly going to confront that man."

During the first visit to the house with Tanous, Campbell tape-recorded the entire experience. When she listened to the tape afterward, she found that it was obscured by "a series of unidentified clicking sounds" that rendered it almost unintelligible.

Armed once again with tape recorder Campbell and Tanous paid a second visit to the house in late November of 1982, hoping, she said ,"that the proximity to the one hundredth anniversary of Beckett's death would prompt stronger vibrations. It did."

Tanous and Campbell wandered about the house, choosing the room in which to encounter the ghost. Tanous selected the living room, and he and Campbell, plus witnesses Veronica and Robert Kenney, settled there in the half light with the shutters closed waiting for the ghost. Tanous had been sitting on the windowsill quietly for only a few minutes when he turned and said, "He's here."

Suddenly, they heard three heavy knocks coming from the next room. They knew that there was no one else in the house with them at the time. Nonetheless, they checked the room where they had heard the knocking and found it empty. They returned to the living room, where Tanous again was silent until, as Campbell reports, "in a voice and manner very unlike his own," he began to speak.

"I was always raised to believe that there was no separation from those who passed on and those who remain," said Tanous (Beckett?). "Much of my writing reflects this because people would not understand what I was saying. You have asked why I stay here. Why should I leave that which I love most? It does not take away from my new life but rather enhances it, since you people believe so differently than I do. But then again, it is not a belief. The difference is that you are there and I am here. . . ."

Tanous, still in a trance, went on to say that during the latter part of his (Beckett's) life, he was thought of as "eccentric." Indeed, Beckett's obituary points out that his mind had been going toward the end.

Skepticism, apparently, is something that spirits do not easily tolerate. Campbell had been doubtful about the whole visit, and during Tanous's trance she suddenly succumbed to an uncontrollable coughing fit that forced her to leave the room. But this was not the only strange manifestation the group experienced. While Tanous was speaking, Veronica found that her pen would not write, but as soon as he finished, it worked fine. When Campbell listened to the recording she had made, she noted that the knocking they had heard was absent from the tape. Also, static had once again obscured the section of tape recorded during Tanous's trance, although his voice had recorded clearly after he came out of the trance. Tanous later speculated that Beckett's spirit had detected Campbell's doubt and had caused the pen failure as well as the obliterated section of tape.

The current owner of the house says that she does not believe in ghosts. She says that nothing out of the ordinary has happened there for a long time. She did relate one instance in which an outside door leading to the tower opened by itself. A landscape worker noticed that a blue curtain was billowing out the door, and he went inside to investigate. When he got to the house, he realized that there was no blue curtain at all.

The owner believes that with all the renovating she has done to Beckett's Castle, if there were any ghosts there, she has driven them out.

"Perhaps they just don't like to bother me," she offers.

Yet Alex Tanous feels that there are still many spirits there, gathering as they did in this world, around the welcoming and inspiring presence of Sylvester Beckett.

14

Abernathy

Linda Campana's children came to know Abernathy long before he made himself known to anyone else. Linda is a creative person by nature and soon after she and her family moved into the old eighteenth-century house on Sheepscot Road in Newcastle, she amused her children with stories of a little boy ghost that playfully haunted the place. If a room felt unusually warm, Linda told them that it was Abernathy's "flaming red hair" irradiating the space. If one of their shoes or a toy or a piece of clothing was misplaced, Linda said that it was the mischievous Abernathy playing a trick on them, though she was thinking all the while that they had simply been negligent with their property, as children are prone to be. The children came to believe in the little ghost with the red hair that blazed like fire, and they even grew comfortable with the thought of having him around to keep them company. It wasn't until Linda decided to do some research on the house that she realized her tales of Abernathy may have been much closer to fact than fiction.

Linda was in the county courthouse one day, researching the deeds to her house. She found that she and her husband were only the fourth owners. The original family, named Woodbridge, had built the place in the late 1700s. The

Woodbridges had lived there for a number of years until a tragic accident occurred. A fire broke out and two of the Woodbridge children died in the blaze; one was a little boy by the name of Abernethy.

"I stood there in the courthouse as the color drained from my face," remembers Linda. "I had never known anything about the previous occupants of the house. The name Abernathy had just come to me. I was in a state of shock."

But Linda's shock was far from over. One of the reasons she was researching the house was that she and her husband were doing some remodeling and wanted to know more about the original layout. They had torn apart one of the downstairs front rooms, and when they had completely stripped it, they decided to take a photo of the room so that they might compare "before and after" stages of their work.

"A friend of mine who is a photographer was there that day," remembers Linda, "and she took a shot of one wall where the fireplace was. She had a darkroom at her house and developed the film that same day. She returned to me immediately with the pictures because she had found something strange in the photo."

There were no unusual shadows in the room that day. Nothing on the walls, nothing in the corners, no one in the windows to cast a shadow into the room. Yet there they unmistakably were—two wispy, outlined figures of a man and a woman standing against the wall.

"The man was about five-foot-eight or five-nine, and the woman was about five-two," says Linda. "They looked sort of like X-rays. It was very bizarre. We couldn't believe our eyes."

To be sure, Linda's friend photographed the wall again. She quickly developed the film and found the figures still standing there complacently, one on either side of the fireplace.

After this remarkable incident, Linda believed that her house was truly haunted. As more and more unusual things began to happen, Linda increasingly attributed them to Abernathy or perhaps to his ghostly companions. Yet she confesses that she and her family felt oddly protected by Abernathy. The children were not afraid of him, and Linda insisted that he was a happy ghost. Apparently, Abernathy was particularly taken with Linda and her family.

"There were a couple of rooms in the house where guests would not feel comfortable," she states. "The parlor was always cold, even in the hottest weather. We used to go in there in the summer to cool off. There was also a guest room that people felt odd in. They would wake in the middle of the night, sensing that someone else was there in the room. Sometimes Abernathy would hide one shoe on them or something like that. He had a real sense of humor."

One summer, Linda and her husband came as close as she recalls to seeing Abernathy. They were working in the back yard when they both, for no apparent reason, simultaneously looked up at the kitchen window. There was a figure looking out at them through the glass. He wore a white shirt that Linda observed was of "an older design." Linda and her husband looked at each other and then back at the window, but the figure had vanished. They inspected the inside of the house and found no one there at all.

The most unsettling experience Linda had with Abernathy happened very late one night when she was at the house alone.

"It was about two or three in the morning," she remembers, "and I had been asleep. I was awakened by the sound of water running downstairs, as if someone were taking a shower. I knew that no one had been in the house when I went to bed, but my nephew was in the habit of staying with us sometimes, and it was not unlike him to get in rather late. I followed the sound of the water to the bathroom downstairs, but when I got there it had stopped. I called out but no one answered. I opened the bathroom door and saw wet spots, like footprints, on the rug. I followed the spots into the guest room and put on the light, but again there was no one there. However, when I looked at the bed I saw the distinct impression of a body on the bedspread—even the pillow was crushed down in the middle as if someone's head had been there. The covers weren't just askew—the impression was deep and heavy. I felt the bed, and it was damp."

Linda contacted her nephew the next day and asked him if he had come to the house that night. He assured her that he hadn't. She asked the members of her family the same thing, and still the answer was no.

Linda and her family sold the house in 1987. She did not tell the new owners about Abernathy and has been hesitant to since.

"I don't think they could handle it," she says with half a chuckle, for after Linda's family moved out, the new owners were plagued with a rash of mischievous and even dangerous problems. The kitchen was almost destroyed one day because of an unaccountable stove fire, the well water became soapy, things went wrong with the wiring, and short circuits were common.

Poor little Abernathy, Linda feels, must miss her and her family very much.

15

The Angry Grandsire

S ome ghosts seem content enough to have a few people about to haunt or pester, but others can be resentful of intruders even to the point of maliciousness. Ellen McKenney and members of her family suffered at the hands of such a spirit in their ancestral home in Bethel. They even believed the ghost to be one of their own kin.

Ellen's great-grandfather had purchased an old cape in Bethel in the 1800s and had torn it down to build a magnificent Victorian structure. Ellen recalls how, as a teenager in the early 1970s, she felt frightened in certain parts of the house—one poorly lit hallway in particular. Her brother teased her about being afraid of the long, dark hallway, yet Ellen's fears were substantial. It was quite late one night when she was forced to confront those fears—as well as something else.

"I remember having to go to the bathroom in the middle of the night," she recalls. "As I walked down the hallway, I began to feel the hair on the back of my neck rise. Then, suddenly, I saw a figure floating at the end of the hall. It was an old man, wearing farmer's clothes—but they were of an older type, like from the nineteenth century. It was his face that was frightening, though. It was an angry face, all strained and wrinkled. He was screaming at me, but there was no sound coming from his mouth. Another strange thing about it was, I recognized the face from old pictures we had in the house. It was my great-grandfather."

Although Ellen was both shocked and frightened, she had the composure to simply tell her great-grandfather's ghost to "go away," and it did. Her story was received with mixed feelings by her family, and Ellen never witnessed the ghost again. This was not to say, however, that the spirit of her elder relative had abandoned the house he had constructed a century ago.

Some years later, when guests were staying at the house, Ellen's mother gave up her room so that they might be more comfortable. She slept instead in the bedroom off the hallway, which once had been Ellen's great-grandfather's. It was also the room in which he died.

In the middle of the night, Ellen's mother woke to the sensation of being choked. She struggled to get out of bed, but felt balked by some forceful presence. Finally, she freed herself from the invisible grip and got out of the room quickly. She spent the rest of the night on the couch and would never stay in that particular room again.

After Ellen married, she and her husband had occasion to stay in the haunted bedroom. Her husband was awakened one night by the same choking feeling. He was not a believer in spirits, says Ellen, so he simply grunted the feeling off and rolled over to go back to sleep.

Members of Ellen's family still live in the house in Bethel. None have had any more experiences with the angry grandsire, yet the image of his silent, screaming face has remained with Ellen McKenney to this day.

Haunted
Places
and
Objects

16

An Unusual Legacy

I t was an erratic and persistent thumping in the walls that drove Marlborough Packard, of Waterboro, to action. But it wasn't simply the thumping, which would occur at any time, day or night, that Mr. Packard found so astonishing; it was the fact that the thumping followed him and his family to four different houses. In the end, Mr. Packard came to realize that house ghosts weren't specifically his problem—rather, he was in possession of a haunted piece of furniture.

The Packard family had been in Maine since the early 1700s. In the mid-1800s, one of the Packards married a member of the Fleet family from Long Island, New York. Along with the dowry came a brand-new pier table of the Empire period. The table stood about three and a half feet high and was delicately but simply decorated, with a marble top and a mirror attached to the back. Generally used as a serving piece, a pier table was often placed between two windows, a space sometimes referred to as a "pier," hence the name.

In the late 1950s, Mr. Packard inherited the table and kept it stored in a garage. After he married, he moved into a two-family house on Long Island and the table took up residence in a hallway. Not long afterward, the Packards began to hear strange thumping sounds in different parts of the house, as if someone were banging the palm of his hand against the inside of the wall.

One night the sound was so pronounced it woke Mr. and Mrs. Packard from their sleep. At the urging of his wife, Packard got out of bed to try to locate the source of the thumps. Each time he would approach its location, the sound would mysteriously move away, and Packard went so far as to pursue the noise into the attic. Despite his attempts, Packard failed to discover just what was causing the thumping. The following day, he mentioned the incident to the neighbors who lived on the other side of the house. He had talked to them about the noise in the past, and they had said that it might have been caused by a closet door in their bedroom that had to be shut with some force.

"You folks must have been having quite a time over there last night," Packard said to his neighbors.

When they asked him what he was talking about, Packard told them about the thumping, making hopeful reference to the noisy closet door. The surprised neighbors told Packard that they couldn't have been the cause, since they were not at home that night.

Packard and his family finally moved to another part of New York State, this time to a house made of cinderblock. The table, naturally, went with them. They hadn't been in their new place for even a week when the thumping started up again. Sometimes loud, sometimes subtle, it still continued. The Packards moved once again, this time to Waterboro, Maine. The table was placed in the new house, and during their five-year tenure there, the Packards again heard the thumpings in the wall.

"I checked everywhere in that house, from the basement to the attic, and I still couldn't find out what was causing the noise. It was really beginning to get ridiculous," says Mr. Packard.

Finally, the Packards built a brand-new house in Waterboro.

"An hour after we moved in that thumping started up again," states an exasperated Mr. Packard. "We just couldn't believe it."

It was by literal process of elimination that Marlborough Packard realized it was not the houses that were haunted, but rather the pier table he had brought with him. He had noticed one unusual thing about the table in the past. Underneath, on the rough, unfinished wood, was a signature in pencil, presumably that of the table's maker. The signature was illegible, and it had another very peculiar characteristic—sometimes it was there and sometimes not.

"I could usually find it," says Packard, "but when other people looked, sometimes it just wasn't there."

Before realizing that the table and the thumping were in any way related, Packard gave the piece of furniture to a local antiques dealer on consignment. After a year, the dealer decided to buy the table from Packard and put it in his own house. The thumping at the Packard home had ceased the day the table left the premises. When Packard happened to run into the antiques dealer one day, he asked after the table. The pier table's new owner said, "Oh, the table's fine. But, I'll tell you, there have been the weirdest sounds going on in my home lately—like footsteps or thumping. I can't figure it out."

17

The Haunted Mill

Oxford County is the site of numerous mills, both operative and retired. Some of them are over one hundred years old and sometimes several generations of the same family have worked there. For a working man and his family, a mill can become almost a personified benefactor, putting food on the table and clothing on the children's backs. Special relationships can even develop between mill worker and job site. Such was the case with one mill along Route 302 in the Norway area. Some workers at that mill believe that the spirit of a dead mill worker haunts the place. They believe it because they have seen him, although no one there now knows his name.

In the mills of yesteryear, safety in the workplace was not as large an issue as it is today. Tragic and sometimes fatal accidents occurred, for the heavy machinery could be dangerous to work around if one were not cautious. In the early 1900s, one particular accident occurred at the mill on Route 302 in which a millworker fell from a high place into some of the machinery and was mangled to death.

After a number of years, the mill was closed and eventually abandoned until some out-of-staters bought it and revived it. Not long after the mill resumed operation, workers there began to sense some unexplained presence in the building. Odd little instances would happen, such as tools being misplaced and showing up again in the wrong place; switches thrown that had been shut off; breakdowns occurring when they shouldn't have.

None of these instances posed any real danger; they were more mischievous in nature. They continued without explanation until one day an employee saw an older man in a pair of dungaree overalls—the type of clothing millworkers wore a hundred years ago—calmly strolling about one of the catwalks. The millworker knew the man was not employed there, and when he described the incident to his foreman, he was surprised to learn that there had been no visitors at the mill that day. The presence of the older man in the overalls remained unexplained.

When the man next appeared on the catwalk, several people witnessed his visit. The old man said nothing, but simply appeared noiselessly on the catwalk and then vanished. As there was no possible way for someone to climb up to the catwalk unnoticed nor somehow stay at the mill without being detected, workers came to believe that the old man in the overalls was the spirit of the man who had been killed there years ago. He had liked it there, they thought, and all he was doing was simply visiting the place where he had spent many years of his life. Since the mill had been revived after a long period of abandonment, perhaps the old man was pleased to have people again working the mill and keeping it active. It was also thought that perhaps it was from this particular catwalk that he had fallen to his death, and thus it was here that he would reappear time and time again.

Although some of the millworkers refused to believe that their workplace was haunted, they could not deny the odd feelings they would have at different times—feelings that a presence lingered there. Perhaps the old millworker took particular delight in plaguing these skeptics with his bits of mischief. Even though he may have suffered horribly here once, perhaps his fondness for the mill and his desire to remain there far outweighed the momentary pain of his terrible death.

18

A Friend of
the Family

Many ghosts seem to return to familiar places, places where they were perhaps very happy or particularly sad. Hauntings of this kind aren't necessarily malicious or foreboding—sometimes the spirits of the dead just like to visit this world to see how things are and maybe look in on old friends. This was the case with Ellwood Stowell and Herman Brewer.

Herman Brewer was a retired lighthouse keeper who lived at Porter's Landing in Freeport. He was a big man, over six feet tall, with a large, heavy set of shoulders and frame. A shock of white hair stuck out from beneath his ever-present cap, and his gnarled hands were thick and leathery with work and age. With a slight stoop to his step and a generous laugh, Brewer was a crusty but benign old Yankee, as sturdy and reliable as the lighthouse he had vigilantly tended for so many years.

Like many coastal men, Brewer owned a boat—a little flat-bottomed skiff—which he was in the habit of lending to Ellwood Stowell on many days during the summer. Stowell was a postal worker who lived in Freeport and who owned a little cabin out by Wolfs Neck. Each summer he and his family would stay at the cabin, swimming, fishing, and enjoying a pleasant row on late afternoons in Herman Brewer's skiff. When Brewer died he left the skiff to Stowell, who, along with his family, missed the old man very much.

Five years passed, and the Stowells still returned to the cabin at Wolfs Neck each summer. At the start of one of these summer vacations, while he was unloading the skiff from storage, Stowell happened to knock a chip off the bow of the boat. Although it was unfortunate, such an accident in no way affected the boat's seaworthiness, and Stowell thought little of it.

It was Stowell's habit to check on the boat nightly, just to make sure that it was secure on its mooring. A thick, wet fog was up one night when Stowell walked down the bank to check his boat. As he drew closer, he saw someone moving near the skiff. The person was leaning curiously over the boat, examining the bow and the spot where the chip had been knocked out. Stowell called out to the visitor, who didn't respond, and then he suddenly recognized the cap and the worn, ragged sweater—they were Herman Brewer's. Stowell called out again and tossed a rock toward the boat, hitting its side. Brewer then turned and looked at Stowell before he slipped quietly away into the mist.

Shaken, Stowell returned to the cabin to tell his family what he had seen. He was not a man to believe in the hereafter, but he couldn't doubt what his senses had shown him. He fixed the chip in the bow of Herman Brewer's skiff the next day, and neither he nor anyone in his family was visited by the old man again.

19

The Dagger and the Chair

Maggie Allen and her husband, John, moved into the house on Woodmont Street in Portland in 1978. They bought the place from an elderly man and his sister who had lived there since the early forties.

Maggie and John had gotten rather an interesting deal when they bought the house—it came completely furnished. Many of these furnishings were Victorian-era antiques, rich with cherry wood, scrollwork, statuary, and needlepoint. There were also a good number of religious paintings, such as scenes of the Last Supper. Maggie and John were amused by this bounty and pleased to inherit it. But they had inherited more than some unusual furniture—they had moved in with a houseful of spirits.

The first evidence of hauntings was a sighting by Maggie. It was only her second night in the house, and it occurred in the dining room. She was busy stripping wallpaper when she suddenly saw four people—two nuns and two priests—sitting passively at the long dining table. She was stunned, and when she looked again they were gone. But not for long; this group would appear often, always at the table, always stiff and silent. John also witnessed the religious quartet sitting there in their habits. Neither he nor Maggie could believe what they had seen, but they couldn't truthfully deny it either.

The spirits revealed themselves to others as well. One evening Maggie and John were entertaining another couple in the living room, which opens into the dining room. All had a clear view of the dining-room table from where they were sitting.

"We were there, just talking," recalls John, "when I suddenly noticed Maggie and my friend's wife staring into the dining room. From the looks on their faces, I had a pretty good idea of what they were seeing. I looked myself, and there they were, the ghosts of the nuns and the priests. Then I looked at my friend, and he apparently didn't see them, because he had this confused look on his face, wondering what the matter was. Suddenly, his wife started to freak out. She insisted on getting out of there fast, so they just left."

These visual manifestations weren't all that Maggie and John had to put up with. During all hours of the night, the couple could hear the spirits wandering through the house creating disturbances.

"They would fling open doors and move stuff around," recalls Maggie, "and we would hear the sound of footsteps on the first floor and on the staircase. It reached a point where we couldn't sleep because the noises were so loud and constant. Finally, one night when I was awakened by this racket, I got angry and went downstairs. I stood in the dining room and said out loud: 'This has to stop! You have got to go.'"

After serving this spiritual eviction notice, Maggie and John decided to put most of the furniture and religious paraphernalia down in the cellar. This move apparently worked, for the noises ceased and the phantom foursome stopped haunting the house on Woodmont Street.

However, Maggie and John hadn't moved all of the antique

furniture into the basement. There was still a thronelike walnut chair, known as an Eastlake, next to the fireplace in the living room. This chair, like the exiled furniture, had come with the house and was very old. It would eventually cause Maggie and John more actual fright than the relatively harmless spirits in the dining room.

"I would see shadows in the chair out of the corner of my eye," says Maggie, who often relaxed on a sofa opposite the piece of furniture. "It was a very drafty spot near that chair. I don't know if it was from the fireplace, but you could sense a coldness in that part of the room. Over the course of about two months, these shadows in the chair became more and more distinct, and I could see that they were forming a person. I didn't know who or what it was, but I got the strong sense that it was evil. One night, I finally decided to confront it. I looked directly at the chair, and there I saw something that terrified me. It was a man in Victorian-era clothing, with a stiff white collar and a black suit. His black hair was slicked back and he wore mutton chops. When I looked at him, he turned and looked right back at me, and then this horrible, evil grin broke out on his face."

Maggie was terrified and quickly left the room. When she looked there later, the man was gone. This was just the beginning of a long, disturbing haunting by this "gentleman" spirit. He appeared many times to Maggie, always at night and always when she was alone. He would always be in the chair when she saw him, and Maggie felt that it must have somehow been special to him in life. Her husband, however, saw him about the house.

"He would just walk in at different times," John remembers. "He stayed in the house for a long time. I recall that one night I was actually having nightmares about him, and I woke up scared. Then I heard a noise at the bedroom door. I looked up and watched it start to open. Having just had the dream, I was expecting to see him standing there, but it was actually my three-year-old son who wanted to come and get in our bed.

When I asked him why, he said that it was because of the 'man' in his room. I said, 'What man?' and he said, 'You know, that man. He's in my room.' He then described the man Maggie had seen in the chair.

"You could tell he had been a gentleman, because of his clothing. It was Civil War–vintage stuff. But there was one strange thing about his costume—he wore a dagger or short sword around his waist, hanging from a belt."

One night, Maggie felt certain that the ghost was determined to use his dagger on her: "He appeared in the chair as usual, when I was sitting on the sofa. Then I watched his hand move up, and in it he had the dagger. He had that horrifying grin on his face, and I ran from the room in absolute terror. This is when I decided that I had had enough and that something must be done."

Maggie contacted a psychic for help. The woman instructed her to recite a chant in a room upstairs, just above the living room. This chant employed a version of the Twenty-First Psalm, punctuated with an appeal to the spirit—an appeal pointing out that he was dead and now had to "go over" to the other side.

"I was reciting this chant upstairs," says Maggie, "and suddenly I heard this male voice screaming on the first floor. I ran down to the living room and saw a pile of ash in the seat of the chair. It was like he had finally realized that he was dead. The pain of this realization caused him to scream. I almost felt sorry for him in a way. I had the sense that something violent had happened to him during his life and that he was just defending himself with the dagger. He was an earthbound spirit who was caught here, caught in the chair. It was the chair, you see, and not the house that was haunted."

Soon after this, Maggie and John decided to move. A short while before they left the house, John got a phone call from the psychic who had taught Maggie the chant. Maggie was not home at the time.

"She was upset and kind of nervous," says John. "She

wanted to speak to Maggie because she had something important to tell her about the chair. I asked her what it was, and it took a while before she'd say anything to me. She told me that we hadn't gotten rid of the ghost, that we'd only sent it away for a little while. She said there was something powerful and evil in the house and that we were in trouble if we didn't do something. We had to get rid of the chair, she said. We had to burn it. I told her that we were moving and we would be getting rid of it at auction because it was valuable. This woman was really insistent about burning it, though."

They gave the chair to F.O. Bailey Antiquarians, an appraisal and auction firm in Portland. Even though it was a highly valued, beautiful period piece, it went through four auctions before it was sold. "We thought this was unusual," said Maggie, "since it was a nice piece of furniture. It was as if people just had a sense about it. It ended up selling for a lot less than it was worth."

But who had this chair belonged to, and who was its ghostly occupant? The house on Woodmont Street was built in 1930 by a man named McRae, who lived there for six years. In 1937 it was bought by a clergyman—the Reverend Robert W. Plant. Born in 1855, Plant was a native of New Brunswick. He had been a missionary among the lumbermen of northern Ontario and the cowboys and miners of the Western frontier. (Hard men to preach the gospel to, no doubt.) In 1894 he came to Maine, where he served a parish in Gardiner, and he retired from his pastoral career in 1935 after serving at the Church of St. Mary the Virgin in Falmouth Foreside. He purchased the house on Woodmont Street, and it is probable that the religious items and the ornate furnishings in the place were all his. He fell ill in late summer of 1940, and by mid-October he was dead.

Is it likely, though, that this man of the cloth was the man with the dagger haunting the home of Maggie Allen and her husband? He founded missions, set up a home for needy children, and faithfully served numerous parishes throughout his long, distinguished career as an Episcopal clergyman. It is easier to imagine such a man entertaining some fellow ecclesiastic spirits at a dining-room table than wielding a dagger at a frightened woman.

But a closer look at the Reverend Plant's life reveals that his father had been an army officer. If the Reverend had been born in 1855, his father probably was middle-aged during the Civil War, the era to which Maggie and John felt the spirit in the chair belonged. It would not be unusual for a former military officer to bear a weapon such as a short sword or dagger. Maggie's sense that he had suffered from or at least been involved with violence is also supported by the fact of his having been an army officer.

Finally, the chant the psychic told Maggie to recite was based on Psalm 21, which concerns battles and military strength:

> May your hand reach all your enemies;
>   may your right hand reach your foes!
> Make them burn as though in a fiery furnace,
>   when you appear.
> May the Lord consume them in his anger;
>   let fire devour them. . . .

An appeal, perhaps, to the militaristic nature of this phantom? The allusions to burning and fire may answer the question of the ashes Maggie found in the chair. It is difficult to say.

The current owners of the house on Woodmont Street say that no spirit now haunts the place. When Maggie and her husband moved, they cleaned the house out from top to bottom, and all the furniture was gone. The chair's whereabouts are unknown, and unless it was burned as the psychic had prescribed, its ghostly occupant may be sitting in it, grinning maliciously, at this very minute.

20

The Ghost in the Aisles

Bob and Joanne Perry, owners and operators of the Skowhegan Cinema, bought the place in 1972. With their purchase came the old stuffed theater seats, a lot of gold fretwork, velvet curtains, balconies, and murals—a typical movie palace from the late twenties. What they hadn't expected to find there was a ghost—an angry and quite malicious one at that.

It was the Perrys' plan to convert the upstairs part of the theater into an apartment. They started work on this renovation shortly after purchasing the building. When the renovations began, some very strange things happened, and the Perrys soon believed they were dealing with something very real and very violent. Bob admitted to feeling a little apprehensive about parts of the building. He sensed he was being watched occasionally; at other times he would detect a sharp drop in temperature in certain areas of the aisles. The Perrys' uneasy suspicions eventually compelled them to solicit the help of Leslie Bugbee.

Bugbee is a psychic from the nearby town of Cornville. When he visited the theater to investigate, the Perrys told him of their experiences and said they were hoping he could determine what was going on in their theater.

"It first started with the wiring," related Bugbee. "Bob was working on the ceiling upstairs and got a real bad shock from some wiring there. The power was off—an electrician had shut it off. They called the electrician back and then *he* got shocked, even though the power *was* off.

"Then there was a time when Bob was plastering the ceiling. Suddenly the trowel shook in his hand and leapt right out of it. It came down hard on a counter top and put a dent in the Formica. This shocked Bob quite a bit because Formica is such strong stuff and difficult to dent. Another time during the renovation, Joanne had an unopened can of wood stain in the middle of the floor. A friend dropped by, and Joanne went downstairs to greet her. When the two went back up to the apartment, they saw a roll of masking tape lift up and roll across the floor at them. It stopped at their feet, and then they looked up and saw the wall."

Wood stain was splattered across the freshly painted wall. The can in the middle of the room was untouched, however, and had apparently remained so while Joanne had been greeting her friend. Bob had not gone near it, and the lid was still sealed. Yet the splotches on the wall were very real. Joanne remarked that it was as if an angry child had been in the room and had just thrown the stain at the wall.

Despite these instances, the Perrys went ahead with their renovations and continued to show movies in the theater. Although most of the disturbances took place in the upstairs apartment, there were indications that the theater space itself was haunted. During a showing of one of the "Halloween" series films, a large piece of plaster from above the balcony came loose and fell into the aisle. It happened to land in front of some people who were being rowdy at the time. No one was hurt by the accident.

Whatever was causing disturbances here could be mischievous as well as violent. Bob Perry used to keep firewood stacked neatly in a back room off the theater. One day he entered the room to find his woodpile rearranged in an odd way: the front of the stack was still piled straight up, but the logs from the rear had been taken out and laid, end to end, across the floor. In fact, there wasn't a square inch of floor space left for him to walk on. A practical joke? Perhaps. But surely a most ambitious one.

For psychic Leslie Bugbee, all this added up to the strong possibility that there was a spirit here who resented what the Perrys were doing to the theater. As we have seen, renovating an old building is one of the surest ways to anger and agitate spiritual entities, and Bugbee believed that the ghost haunting the Skowhegan Cinema was either a person who had worked in the theater or who had lived in a house that once stood on the property.

One method Bugbee has used to communicate with spirits is through tape recordings. Just as the image of a ghost may linger in a house, says Bugbee, so may its voice remain. It is his belief that you can record messages from spirits such as tapping, breathing and whispers. He calls this EVP, or electronic voice phenomenon.

During Bugbee's investigation of the Skowhegan Cinema, he recorded the silence of the theater's empty interior several times. On one tape, he and the Perrys detected some tapping noises that none had heard when the tape had been rolling. Bugbee also sensed that the spirit of Bob Perry's mother was in the theater, perhaps just visiting her son. Other alleged messages from beyond were manifested during the investigation. Bugbee had brought along a photographer, but when he got inside the theater, none of his equipment would work. When he went back outside to check it, the equipment worked fine. When he was inside the theater, though, it failed again.

The Perrys say that strange things still happen at their theater. Day or night, they are plagued by the feeling that some kind of presence is there. If this spirit follows the path of other ghosts, it may eventually become used to the rearrangements at the cinema and haunt the Perrys no more; however, there have been instances in which an angry spirit has stubbornly stayed on to make its presence known and its hostility felt. In such a battle of wills between the spiritual and the corporeal, one usually has to outlast the other. The Perrys have no idea how long their ghost will persist, but they apparently intend to stay.

AUTHOR'S NOTE: Bob and Joanne Perry were unwilling to talk to me about their experiences at the Skowhegan Cinema. The material for this chapter was gleaned primarily from interviews with Leslie Bugbee and from a November 1984 article in Yankee magazine by Mike Kimball. Kimball accompanied Bugbee while the psychic was investigating the cinema.

21

The Ghostly Campus

S equestered in the northwestern part of the state, in the foothills of Saddleback and Sugarloaf mountains, the University of Maine at Farmington has known many distinguished alumni during its history. Politicians, professors, and important educational reformers (the university was originally a school for teachers) have all known its lovely, ivy-covered brick buildings. Those same buildings have also been home to a spirit or two.

Campus rumor has it that one dormitory, Purington Hall, is haunted by the ghost of a housemother said to have hanged herself there many years ago. School authorities scoff at this story, saying that Purington never had a housemother, yet the rumors persist. It was in the fall semester of 1979, however, that the suspicions about Purington shifted to its neighbor, Mallett Hall.

Mallett, a women's dormitory, had been the scene of several campus police investigations owing to unexplained noises in the attic. Footsteps had been heard coming from behind locked doors, sounds so loud and insistent that two students actually moved out of a room below.

A college prank? Perhaps. Yet campus police took note of how difficult, if not impossible, it would have been for someone to get into that attic and how ambitious he or she would have to be to keep the prank going for so long. Not long after, however, the prankster moved out of the attic and right into the bedroom of two students.

It was about 2:00 a.m. when two women on the third floor heard a loud noise in the center of their room. It sounded as if someone had lifted the desk there and dropped it. They got up to investigate but could find no one else in the room. It was hard for them to believe they were both having the same incredible dream, and this hopeful theory was totally dispelled the next morning when a student who lived in the room below theirs asked them what they had dropped on the floor in the middle of the night.

Several nights later, only one of the roommates was sleeping in the dorm room. She was in the bottom bunk, and about 4:00 a.m. she was awakened by the sound of movement in the bunk above her. She thought that it might be some of her friends trying to play a joke on her, but then she noted that the upper mattress was not sagging at all. This was when she became frightened and decided to just lie still, hoping that whoever or whatever it was would go away.

Then she heard whispers coming from the bunk. She listened closely, and soon recognized that it was her name being spoken in a slow and deliberate voice. She finally summoned the courage to put on the light beside her bed and flee for the door without looking back. She wouldn't return to the room for the rest of the night, and it took some doing to get her to go back, let alone stay there, again.

The last straw for both roommates came when a rocking chair in the room took to rocking back and forth by itself. When they couldn't stand it any longer, they sought the help of a psychic, Kay Mora, who had attended the university and gone on to teach two courses there in psychic awareness.

Mora, with an audience of some twenty spectators, visited the dorm room and within minutes picked up signs of the presence of a ghost. She told everyone that the ghost was there, and then sensed that it was leaving because it was unused to crowds. She convinced the ghost that they wanted it to stay for a while so they could communicate.

Through telepathy, Mora began to get a picture of what had happened and who the spirit was. Her name was Edith, said the psychic, and she had been a student at the university a long time ago. She had been in an automobile accident, killed instantly in the crash. She was engaged to be married at the time of her death, and Mora suspected that her betrothed was still in Farmington somewhere. Edith had happy memories of her student life at UMF, and this, said Mora, was why she was staying there at Mallett. According to the psychic, Edith was simply unable to accept the fact that she was really dead.

Mora was experienced at helping ghosts "get to the other side," and used her skills to persuade the ghost of Edith to leave Mallett Hall. After this, students in Mallett were reportedly not bothered any longer by restless spirits and could concentrate on their studies.

While one dormitory might have been freed of its ghost, there was yet another supposedly haunted room on campus—Nordica Auditorium, named in honor of Farmington's most famous daughter, Lillian Nordica.

Madame Lillian Nordica, this country's premier opera singer of the nineteenth century, had toured the world singing for presidents, kings, and czars. She was born Lillian Bayard Norton in 1857 in Farmington, the sixth daughter in a musically talented and religious farming family. Her gift went unrecognized at first, but with the death of an older sister whom her family had been training to be a singer, Lillian stood out as a young girl who showed much promise. The legends surrounding the early life of little Lillian Norton have her wandering in the forests of her rural home, sweetly trilling to the birds in the trees.

Sparrows were not to remain her exclusive audience. When her mother and her music teacher realized what talent Lillian had, they whisked her off to the New England Conservatory of Music in Boston. From here she was taken under the wing of an older Italian opera dame who introduced her to New York stages. Her opera coach thought that her name would be unpronounceable to Italian audiences, so he gave her the stage name of Nordica, which was Norton loosely Italianized. After this, Nordica's career took off, leading her to such cultural and operatic centers as Rome, London, and St. Petersburg, where she sang for the delight of Czar Alexander II.

Although she became an incomparable star, Lillian did not forget her origins and returned to Farmington several times to give performances. The last of these took place in 1911 in Merrill Hall, a large, red-brick Italianate structure. The concert was in the second-floor auditorium, a beautifully designed space with high ceilings, gilded fretwork, and tall, elegant windows. This space was later renamed Nordica Auditorium.

Today Nordica Auditorium is the center of activities for the music department, with concerts and recitals held there on a regular basis. But some say there is more going on in Nordica Auditorium than student recitals. In the late hours of the evening, usually close to midnight, when the building is dark and quiet and the five hundred seats in the auditorium are empty, a mellifluous soprano voice has been heard echoing in the hall. It has been talked about by students, alumni, and faculty alike, and all have ventured that the voice belongs to none other than Madame Lillian Nordica.

In the fall of 1988, Kelly Nelson and her friend Micky Tolkinen were passing through Farmington on their way to the Sugarloaf Ski Resort. Micky had heard about the Nordica

Auditorium legend from a former Farmington student and wanted to see the place for himself.

It was the middle of a weekday afternoon, and the auditorium was empty when they got there. Kelly, a musician, was pleased to see a piano in one corner of the auditorium, and she sat down to play while Micky looked about. A tall, formal portrait of Nordica graced one wall, and opposite this was a smaller portrait of her in the character of Isolde, one of her most famous roles. Kelly had taken no note of the portraits, for she was too busy playing her music. With her eyes closed, she began to play a beautiful, rambling, freestyle piece.

"It was full of high notes," she recalled, "and unlike anything I normally played. It was like I wasn't there for a few moments."

She continued to play while Micky wandered about the auditorium, feeling, somehow, that they were not actually alone. He looked up to the tall Nordica portrait and felt that Lillian Nordica's spirit would indeed be pleased to be in a place where she could always hear music.

Suddenly Kelly stopped playing. As the resonant, final chords of the piano faded, Kelly opened her eyes and said, "Did she wear a lot of blue?"

The question took Micky by surprise. He asked Kelly what she meant. The color, she said, had been filling her mind as she played, and it came through to her in an extremely strong image.

Micky, who had been sitting in one of the seats as he listened, rose and took Kelly's hand. He walked her down the side aisle and up to the portrait of Nordica as Isolde. There, with her full, smiling lips and luxuriant brown hair, was Nordica, swathed in a rich sky-blue veil. The color of the veil stood out sharply against Nordica's/Isolde's white gown.

Kelly smiled and put her hands in her pockets.

"I thought I felt someone here," she said, "as if someone were inside of me playing. It was beautiful."

Lillian Nordica died of exposure and pneumonia on May 10, 1914, on an island in Java during what was to be her final world tour. Although she was deathly ill, she insisted on giving her performances, until she was so weak she could no longer stand up on stage.

"A prima donna dies three deaths," she had once said, "when her beauty dies, when her voice dies, and when the breath leaves her body."

If the voice that had brought her worldwide acclaim still rings from the vaulted ceilings of Nordica Auditorium in Farmington, we may say, then, that she has not truly died and is still sharing her beauty and her breath with us.

22

The Haunted High School

Bill Nelson has been a janitor at the Brunswick High School for over ten years, and he would laugh if you were to ask him about the ghost there. His laughter would not be inspired by disbelief, but would be more akin to the chuckle one sometimes gives when remembering an amusing friend. During his long career at Brunswick High, Mr. Nelson has had numerous experiences at the hands of a spirit he calls Mimi. As one teacher at the school points out, the janitors don't like to speak much of Mimi; they are afraid people will think they are crazy or perhaps colluding in an elaborate joke. Yet their stories of the strange noises, the footsteps in the darkness, and the flickering lights have been substantiated by other witnesses on more than one occasion.

Cecelia Termini, secretary to the school's principal, was working in the office one evening in 1984 after everyone else had gone home. She had a big report to prepare for the next day and was busy with her typing and paperwork. Around seven o'clock she stepped into an adjacent room to use the copy machine. As she was turning back, she heard the sudden and distinct sound of books being dropped right in front of her feet. Nothing in the room had fallen as far as she could see, and although she thought it strange, she shrugged it off as lightly as she could.

"It wouldn't have bothered me that much if it had only happened the one time," she says. "But when I went back to make some more copies and started to return to the office, it happened again. That's when the hair on my arms stood up and I decided to get out of there right away. To this day, I have no idea what caused the noise. I don't really believe in ghosts, but I know what I heard. There was no one else in the building that night. I was all alone, and I was scared."

Ms. Termini will no longer work at the high school by herself. Shortly after her experience a senior at the high school was killed in a car accident. Ms. Termini initially did not connect this incident with the events in her office, but has since come to suspect that the two occurrences may strangely be connected. This may be due to what Brunswick High teacher Hugh Dwyer has learned of Mimi.

In late December 1987, Mr. Dwyer happened to be at the school very late at night—or early in the morning, rather, around 1:00 a.m. He had spent the first part of the night at the hospital, where his wife had just given birth to their first child, and he wanted to stop off at the school to prepare some lessons for the next day before going home to bed.

"It was about 1:30 when I was leaving the bulding through the auditorium, which happens to be the oldest part of the school. Just as I was opening the door to leave, I heard the tremendous slam of a door somewhere above me. I had brought my dog, Bear, along with me for company, and his ears pricked up immediately. I felt certain that a door must have been slammed by a draft, because I was almost certain that I was there alone. Then, suddenly, I heard the door again. It was a hard, deliberate slam. Bear took off after the noise, and although I called him back, he wouldn't listen. I followed him upstairs and found him standing perfectly still in the middle of one of the hallways. This was sort of odd, since I was accustomed to having him growl and bark at noises. I thought that since I was up there I had better check things out, so I went around and tried all the doors and found them locked, as they should have been. I walked through the whole building and checked everywhere, but the place was empty. Since it was so quiet, I was sure that if someone had tried to get out of the building after the slamming noises, I would have heard him.

"When I finally left, I remember feeling a real spine chill run up my back as I crossed the threshold. It had snowed while I was there, so, just to be sure, I went around the school checking for any fresh footprints in the snow. There weren't any."

Mr. Dwyer teaches English, and as a writing assignment he told his class about his experiences and had them write up explanations for what had happened. Many of the students interviewed Bill Nelson and the other janitors, and they found out some interesting things.

"Apparently, I wasn't the only one who had had such experiences at the school after hours," says Mr. Dwyer. "My students learned that some of the janitors had witnessed unexplained events—lights would be on, for example, when they had certainly been turned off. Some saw things thrown around the room, baskets overturned, and things like that." Bill Nelson recalled being in the school alone one night and hearing footsteps behind him. When he turned, no one was there.

Through his own research, Mr. Dwyer found out that a number of years ago a female student had fallen from the balcony in the auditorium and died of a broken neck. According to Bill Nelson, the student's name was Mimi. Mr. Dwyer checked back through the yearbooks for a former student by that name, but his search was unsuccessful. The book for 1961 was missing, and he posited that this may have been the year of the girl's death. Another janitor at the school believes that the accident took place long before that, however.

Mr. Dwyer's investigations did lead to some interesting

conclusions. As he thought back on his experiences that night in the auditorium, he recalled that the sounds of the door slamming had come from the area of the balcony from which Mimi was supposed to have fallen. He also noted that Mimi was at her most active whenever something bad happened or was about to happen to a Brunswick High student.

"As I think back on all of this," says Dwyer, "I will never forget the feeling I had that night in the school. I had the relentless sense that there was someone with me. I don't believe in spirits, but I can't deny how I felt or what I heard. I would like to hear an explanation, but I have a sense now of not really being surprised that there could be a Mimi at the school. She's really kind of a friendly spirit."

Haunted
Inns
and
Taverns

23

A Tale
of Murder

This tale of ghostly vengeance is a bit out of the ordinary, as we have a killer haunting the house of his victim's son after the son took revenge upon the killer.

The details of this convoluted story may be said to have begun in 1747 when one Joseph Knight of Windham was captured and held prisoner by Indians. He remained a captive long enough to pick up some of the Indians' language, so in 1756, when he was captured again, he was able to understand what his abductors were talking about. He was shocked to learn that a great ambush was being planned for all the settlements from Brunswick to Saco, and he took the earliest opportunity to escape and warn the settlers of the impending attack.

At that time in Freeport—or North Yarmouth, as it was called—a family by the name of Means lived out on Flying Point, a spit of land that juts into Casco Bay just beyond the Wolfs Neck area. The Means family consisted of parents Thomas and Alice; their children, Jane, Alice, and Robert; Molly Finney, Mrs. Means's sister; and a hired man by the name of Martin. The Means farm was barely a half mile away from the safety of a blockhouse where the other settlers had taken refuge from the inpending attack. For some reason—perhaps because of the proximity of the blockhouse or perhaps because they simply were not prepared to move—the Meanses decided to wait until the following morning to join the others in the stockade. It was one of the last decisions Thomas Means was ever to make for his unfortunate family; shortly before dawn, a party of Micmac Indians attacked their cabin.

Thomas Means was killed immediately and Mrs. Means, holding her infant son Robert in her arms, was shot. The bullet passed through the baby's body and lodged in Mrs. Means's chest, where it remained the rest of her life. The hired man, Martin, had been fumbling in the darkness for his rifle and took a shot at the attacking Indians from the window of his attic room. He managed to wound one of the Micmacs and frighten the others into running away, yet they carried off with them young Alice and her aunt Molly Finney. Alice escaped from her captors after a few hours, but Molly was taken to Canada and sold into servitude.

The remaining members of the Means family got to the blockhouse, where they recovered from their ordeal. Although she was wounded, Mrs. Means survived and after several months in the stockade gave birth to the last child of Thomas Means. This son was named in honor of the father he had never known, and the widow later married one Colonel George Rogers who had been stationed at the garrison.

At the outbreak of the Revolution, eighteen-year-old Thomas Means enlisted as a private soldier in the Colonial forces. Means was an able soldier and fought bravely for his homeland's freedom at many battles, including Ticonderoga, Stillwater, and Saratoga. He was at Valley Forge with General Washington and served under "Mad" Anthony Wayne at the battle of Stony Point. When his enlistment was up in December 1779, he returned to his native town of Freeport, where he was eventually elected to the first board of selectmen and served as town treasurer. By 1807, Means was known as a respectable "gentleman of Freeport" and had earned the sobriquet "Major," probably for his distinguished service during the war. It was said that in the heart of the youth now turned man there still burned the desire for revenge upon the Indian who had taken his father's life. Major Thomas Means of Freeport believed that one day the hand of fate would bring his father's murderer before him so he could avenge the crime committed upon his family so many years before.

In 1807 Major Means purchased a house that stood on the corner of present-day Bow and Main streets in Freeport. The house had belonged to the Reverend Alfred Johnson and had been built for him by the citizens of the town so that they could have their own minister in residence. The Reverend Johnson moved on to Belfast eventually, and Major Means took advantage of the recent glut of economic traffic through Freeport by opening a tavern in the Reverend's former home.

Means's Tavern prospered, as it was located at a major crossroads, and Thomas Means kept the tavern himself, spending long winter nights in the company of other veterans. Before the blazing fire, they drank rum and told tales of the war. One dark and blustery night, the Major was behind the bar while his companions sat across the room. They all turned their heads for a moment when the door of the tavern opened and in stepped a tall, swarthy Indian. Means noticed that there was a slight stagger to his walk and a glowering look in his face. The Indian, dressed in white-man's clothing, made his way to the bar and uttered a single word: "Rum!"

The Major poured his guest a mug of liquor and handed it to him. The Indian drained the mug and asked for more; the Major obliged once again. There was something bleak and mysterious about the Indian, and the other patrons in the bar avoided staring at him as best they could. When he began to speak, though, they couldn't keep their attention to themselves. The big Indian spoke of how he had been a member of a great and powerful war party that had massacred a family near the fort many years ago.

As the Indian revealed each terrible detail of his story, the people in the tavern knew that he was referring to the Means massacre. All eyes turned to Major Means, who had remained silent and impassive behind the bar. He provided his guest with food and more rum—perhaps a little more than the Indian needed—until the man said he was ready to retire. Major Means lit a candle for him and guided the Indian to a cupola on the roof, known as a "monitor room." No one ever saw the Indian come down from the monitor room again. In fact, no one ever heard what became of him, but some must have suspected. They must have known what horrible and powerful thoughts of revenge were swarming through the Major's mind that evening, and they could only imagine what deeds went on in the darkness of that small room above the tavern.

Not long after the arrival and disappearance of the Indian, it was said that Major Means never again enjoyed the benefit of a good night's sleep. The Major's insomnia might not have been due to a sense of guilt as much as it was to the "flashing lights and uncanny sounds" that issued from the monitor room on stormy nights. One dark, wet evening, when the lightning flashed and thunder cracked loudly over the bay and the wind howled about the sturdy walls of the tavern, Major Means saw the figure of the Indian flitting back and forth across the monitor room. The sightings continued, and the Major was almost driven mad with terror. The spirit of the Indian kept up its ghostly vigil above Means's Tavern for many years. When the Major lay on his deathbed in 1828, he made a confession to his son that he had killed the Indian with a hatchet that night in the monitor room, horribly replicating the scalping of Thomas Means in 1756.

The Major's confession apparently was not enough of a

gesture to eradicate the ghost of the Indian, for it was said that the monitor room remained haunted well after Means's death. It wasn't until at least fifty years later, when new owners of the tavern removed the monitor room from the roof, that the spirit of the Indian troubled the inn no longer.

24

The Portrait of a Lady

The Captain Lord Mansion on Pleasant Street in Kennebunkport is a beautiful old Federal-period structure. It
sits high on a hill overlooking the Kennebunk River and a long,
gently rolling lawn known as "the River Green." Built in 1815
by Nathaniel Lord, a prosperous local shipbuilder and merchant (who died the year his splendid house was completed),
the mansion remained in the family primarily through matri-
lineal descent right up until the 1970s. From the Lords to the
Clarks to the Bucklands to the Fullers, the old mansion was
passed down through generations of old Maine families. Over
the years, the house became smaller and smaller, in a way, as
rooms and hallways were shut up or sealed off to accommo-
date the dwindling numbers of Nathaniel Lord's descendants
still living there.

This legacy came to an end in 1972, when the house was
purchased by a speculator named Jim Thromulos. It was when
the house left family hands, some say, that the trouble began at

the Lord Mansion; others say it happened before that. But all agree on one point: the house is most certainly haunted.

When he bought the crumbling old manse, Thromulos planned to restore it to its former glory. To achieve this, he came up with the scheme of inviting a number of talented and artistic young people to move in and work on the place. He succeeded in attracting a dozen or so enthusiastic young men and women to take on the unique project. Together they scraped woodwork, refinished floors, stripped wallpaper, and generally brought the house back into good structural shape. Yet these activities, however well-intentioned, had an unforeseen negative effect.

Tom Glassman was one of the first to suspect that something unusual was happening in the Lord house. He was staying in a downstairs front room known as the "wedding, wake, and baptism" room, or the music room. Above the fireplace in his room was a portrait of Sally (Clark) Buckland, a fifth-generation granddaughter of Captain Nathaniel Lord. An august, handsome woman, Sally had loved the old mansion and spent many happy summers there with her husband, Edward, and her family during the early 1900s. The portrait showed a woman in her late forties with gray hair, a proud, erect chin, and the slightest suggestion of a smile.

"Everyone was bothered by that portrait," remembers Glassman. "The eyes would follow you wherever you walked."

Glassman was working in the room one day when he suddenly noticed an old man standing there looking at the painting. Glassman was startled because he hadn't heard the man come into the house or enter the room. Nevertheless, he began to chat with the man, who looked back at the portrait and said, "That's my aunt."

"I turned to do something," recalls Glassman "and while my back was to him for just a second, he was gone—just as quickly and quietly as he had shown up." Glassman never heard from or saw the man again.

The mysteries of the mansion came to baffle not only the eye, but the nose as well. In the process of restoring the thirty-eight rooms of the house, numerous chemical strippers and paints were used that had very strong odors. Not wanting to cause a health hazard, Glassman and his companions often left windows opened wide so that fresh air would circulate. Even with strong outdoor breezes and noxious chemical fumes permeating the mansion, there yet remained a horrible smell that anyone visiting the house would comment on.

"Rotting fish," says Glassman. "It was very powerful. It came and went the whole time we were restoring the place."

While the youthful tenants of the Lord Mansion grew accustomed to this obnoxious smell, other fantastic evidence of a ghostly presence was revealed to them. On one particular night, Sally Buckland's portrait was responsible for inspiring more than simple uneasiness.

"I was in the music room with two women friends, drinking brandy," says Glassman. "We had the windows shut, but we could still feel a cold breeze. Then the portrait started to look like it was glowing, and laserlike lights began shooting around the room and in and out of the portrait. We all saw this and were amazed. I had a radio in the room as well as a record player, and they both began to go on and off by themselves. The lights started to do the same thing. There was nothing but static coming over the radio, and I thought to myself that perhaps what was happening was a bad connection or current somewhere in the house. But in order for that record player to start playing, someone would have had to physically lift up the tonearm and turn on the switch. None of us had."

This was too much for the young Glassman, who had previously labeled himself a "pragmatist and a disbeliever" in spirits. He decided to visit an occult shop in Kennebunk to get some answers. There he was told that a ghost (probably that of Sally Buckland) had driven the last family of Lord descendents out of the house and was now attempting to do so to Glassman and his friends.

"The guy at the shop told me that the fish smell was a fairly common way ghosts have of getting rid of peope," says Glassman. "He said that Sally Buckland had really loved the place and loved living there in Kennebunkport. She had been a prominent member of the community and had founded a garden club. She was very attached to the gardens at the mansion, and especially to the house itself. She was so fussy about it that she used to make her children walk up the sides of the staircase so they wouldn't step on the Oriental runner. She just didn't want to leave the place. The man at the shop advised me to try and make her happy by convincing her that we were all there to preserve the house, not to ruin it or invade it."

Glassman's report of this to the others was received largely with amusement. Some of those living in the house suspected that something was wrong, but most simply attributed the strange happenings to coincidence or imagination. The most ardent disbeliever, says Glassman, was owner Jim Thromulos, yet even he got a taste of Sally Buckland's displeasure and territorialism.

Intending to sand the floors in the music room one night, Thromulos changed his mind when a window shade suddenly snapped up as he crossed the threshold.

"He was generally a hard-working guy," recalls Glassman. "It was unusual for him to start on a job and then not see it through. But he said that he just got a weird feeling in there. He was also not one to believe in ghosts, so that made it more unusual."

One person who swears the portrait of Sally Buckland not only stared at him but actually prevented him from entering a room was Paul Dahm.

"It was toward Halloween," remembers Dahm, who often spent time at the mansion visiting friends, "and I thought this might be a good time to approach her. It was around midnight when I started walking down the hallway toward the room where the portrait was. But I backed off because I started to feel this tremendous force against my body. I just got the sensation that I should get out of there right away, which I did."

On several occasions, people heard footsteps in different parts of the house. With so many persons living there, this might not seem like such a strange phenomenon, but footsteps don't usually travel through walls.

"I remember being in the dining room one night with another guy who lived there, named Cliff," Glassman says. "We heard footsteps upstairs going back and forth, back and forth. We were both busy reading and we ignored it at first, thinking that it must have been someone else who lived there. But soon we both realized something: the footsteps were going from room to room, but they weren't going out into the hallway like they would have to in order to do this. Instead, they were going right through the walls, along the side of the building. We also realized something else: we were the only ones in the house."

The closest Glassman or any of the other tenants ever got to Sally Buckland seems to have been one night during a fierce winter storm. Glassman, a resident named Mary McCullough, and some others decided to go up into the large cupola to watch the snow fall. To their knowledge, no one else was in the house at the time. Suddenly a tree fell and struck a power line, blanketing the mansion in darkness. Glassman volunteered to go down to his room to get an old-fashioned oil lamp he owned. The others followed him out of the cupola and were waiting for him on the third-floor landing. Glassman was at the foot of the stairs when he heard Mary McCullough ask, "Whose light is that?" They all looked where she indicated and saw the light of a lamp move from the dining room to the music room. The light moved in a direct line—right through the walls. Mary screamed, and the light was gone.

"That one really scared us all," admits Glassman.

In 1978 the Lord Mansion was sold to Rick Litchfield and his family, who continued the restoration of the house and turned it into an elegant inn. The Litchfields lived there at first and said that they had no problems there but some of their guests had things to report.

"We had a couple from New Jersey staying upstairs in the Lincoln Room," says Litchfield, who has named all the rooms after ships built by Nathaniel Lord. "They were a young couple, newlyweds, and the wife had been referred to us by her boss, who had stayed at the mansion once with his wife. There was a rocking chair in the room, over by the fireplace.

"In the middle of the night, the wife woke up and saw a young woman sitting in the rocking chair, wearing a nightgown and cap. Then the rocking chair floated across the room, and as it did the woman in it got older and older, until she was an old lady. The wife woke her husband, but by then the chair was back in its usual place and the old lady had disappeared."

The final strange twist in this story is that when the new bride got back to New Jersey and told her boss and his wife what she had seen, she was surprised to learn that her boss's wife had had the very same vision in the Lincoln Room. In both instances, it was only the woman who had seen the girl/old lady in the rocking chair.

"There was a time of turmoil here when this house was sold back in 1972," says Litchfield. "It had been in one family for a long time. Julia Fuller, Sally Buckland's daughter, had tried to maintain the house the way Sally had loved and cared for it. The last family member to live here didn't like the house very much and wanted to get rid of it. There is a portrait of Julia in the dining room, and I understand that every time the family member walked into this room, she could smell rotting fish. I suppose the ghosts of Julia and Sally were upset because they knew the place was going to be sold."

"The house was so nice," recollects Tom Glassman. "I could see how Sally didn't want to leave there."

25

The Ghostly Night Watchman

The Kennebunk Inn, on Main Street in Kennebunk, was built in 1799 and was originally the private home of one Phineas Cole. Ownership passed through several different families during the 1800s, and in 1926 the house became an inn known as The Tavern. The Tavern in turn became the Kennebunk Inn in 1940, and by 1978 it had fallen into disrepair. This was the year that Arthur and Angela LeBlanc purchased the place with visions of restoring it, which they did. This was also the year that the ghost checked in.

"It was about eight years ago," recalls Angela LeBlanc, "when a waitress of ours named Patty had to go down into the basement to get some food. She came back up and said to me in all seriousness, 'Angela, there's a presence down there.' She named this presence 'Cyrus.' She said it was just a name that came to her. She really believed in this stuff, but I didn't at the time, so we all just laughed it off, thinking it was kind of cute. But Patty refused to go into certain parts of the basement. Then things started happening to my staff."

These "things" happened particularly to waitress Janet Cipriani and a bartender named Dudley. The bar at the Kennebunk Inn featured little hand-carved mugs for specialty drinks. They were kept on a shelf behind the bar, but they didn't always stay there. At any time, an errant mug might fly off the shelf and hit Dudley while he was working. Mugs wouldn't just fall off the shelf, but actually flew through the air with considerable force, as if they had been physically hurled by someone. In addition to this rare occupational hazard, Dudley would have to contend with glasses suddenly shattering when no one was anywhere near them.

Janet Cipriani also had some trouble with glasses. "One day I was clearing a table," she recalls, "and I had a tray of very expensive crystal goblets in my hands. I was bringing this into the kitchen and I heard the chef and the dishwasher joking around and telling stories about Cyrus. I told them that I didn't believe in any of this stuff, and that I had never felt or heard anything. Just a few seconds after I said this, one of the crystal goblets flew up in the air and smashed against the wall opposite me. The goblet could have just tipped over and broken on the tray, but it didn't. It lifted right up off the tray, and the other goblets were not knocked over or touched. I was a lot less skeptical after this incident."

Other things plagued Janet. After she and the wait staff would set up tables at night for breakfast the next day, they would arrive to find the tables and chairs askew and the silverware moved about. But Cyrus didn't stop at pestering the staff. He had a certain fondness for two particular rooms in the inn—numbers 7 and 11. Guests staying in these rooms would sense a presence or experience quirky little things.

"One time a guest who was staying in number 7 saw his door keep opening during the middle of the night, even though it had been locked. He said that he kept closing the door but finally had to just leave it open all night," says Angela.

Until this time, Cyrus had remained a mysterious, mischievous, impetuous presence who also roamed the basement of the old inn, tipping over a box here, frightening a waitress there, and generally being a mild nuisance. Yet who or what Cyrus was remained unknown—until a series of events painted a clearer picture of the shadowy, otherworldly inn guest whose name did *not* appear on the register.

"The newspaper ran an article about the ghost here at the inn and identified it as Cyrus," says Angela. "It was read by Priscilla Perkins Kenney, who lives here in Kennebunk. She came to us and told us all about her father, *Silas* Perkins, who had lived in Kennebunk for years."

The similarity of the names "Cyrus" and "Silas" was too uncanny for the LeBlancs and their employees. Something was causing disturbances there at the inn, and they came to believe that it was the ghost of Perkins, the night watchman.

Priscilla Kenney says that she and her family like to think of her father as "the poet of Kennebunk and Kennebunkport"—and with good cause. In addition to being a night watchman and running a coal business for most of his life, Silas Perkins had been a published poet of some worth. His work, appearing in Portland and Boston newspapers, had been admired by such distinguished local literati as Booth Tarkington and Kenneth Roberts. Perkins self-published three collections of his poetry; perhaps his most well known work was "The Common Road." This poem was so popular in its day that it was broadcast on a national radio hookup from the funeral train of President Franklin D. Roosevelt.

Silas used to write his poetry while spending his days in the coal office in Kennebunkport. Although he enjoyed chatting with visitors, he assured himself of a writer's privacy by sawing an inch or two off the front legs of the guest chair in the coal office so visitors wouldn't stay too long. He spent his last years working at the Kennebunk Inn as night watchman/ clerk/auditor. The basement, where the furnace sat and many of the tools were kept, would have been his domain, and probably he spent time sitting in a warm corner, scribbling his poems. In June 1952, when he was seventy-two years old, Silas walked out the front door of the inn one day and crossed the street to buy a newspaper. Before he had made it to the other sidewalk, he had a heart attack. He died that same day in a room at the inn.

"My father spent the last eight years of his life at the inn," says Kenney. "I'd rather like to think that his spirit is still there. He would be a friendly presence. I'm sure of it."

Silas's activities at the inn have never really been unfriendly. What seems more likely is that he was bothered by the flurry of activity that came with the LeBlancs in 1978. When they started their renovations and breathed life back into the crumbling old inn, Silas apparently wanted to let them know that he was there too. Prior to this time, no one could recall a spirit haunting the Kennebunk Inn.

The LeBlancs and the staff, as well as their guests, soon got used to the idea of Silas being around. Angela's daughter Alyse even decided that she at least ought to try to talk to him, "just to see if he liked" her family.

"We made contact with him on a Ouija board once," she says. "When we asked him if he liked us, he went immediately to the 'yes' answer, and that made all of us feel a lot better. Our hands were not pushing the little triangular pointer, yet you could feel it moving. Your hands would be following it, and that's what was so strange about the whole thing. I didn't want to go into it much further at that point. The ghost is definitely in the inn. I consider him to be a friend because to consider him anything else makes me a little nervous. He's a nice ghost—what can I say?"

Acknowledgments
and Sources

T he author wishes to acknowledge his use of the following books, periodicals, and journals in the writing of the chapters listed below.

"The Flying Dutchman of Maine"

Henry Paper, "Portland's Famous Ghost Stories," *Greater Portland* 30, no. 5 (Fall 1985).

E.C. Plummer, "The Privateer *Dash*," *New England Magazine* 10, no. 5 (July 1894).

Florence G. Thurston, *Three Centuries of Freeport* (Portland, Me.: Anthoensen Press, 1940.

"The Curse of the Saco River"

Elizabeth Audie, *A Folklore History of Saco Bay* (Portland, Me.: House of Falmouth, 1976).

Complete Poetic Works of John Greenleaf Whittier, The (Boston: Houghton Mifflin Co., 1895).

Roy P. Fairfield, *Sands, Spindles and Steeples—A History of Saco, Maine* (Portland, Me.: House of Falmouth, 1956).

George Folsom, *History of Saco and Biddeford*, (Saco, Me.: Alex C. Putnam, 1830).

Richard Hallett, "Saco River Outlives Indian Curse," *Portland Sunday Telegram* (29 June 1947).

Daniel Owen, *Old Times in Saco* (Saco, Me.: Biddeford Times Print, 1891).

Estelle Tatterson, *Three Centuries of Biddeford—An Historical Sketch* (pamphlet in collection of the Maine Historical Society).

"Saco River Bears an Old Curse Which Has Been Fulfilled Yearly Since 1675," *Portland Sunday Telegram* (26 July 1931).

"One Foot on the Grave"

Babcock, Blakely B., *Jonathan Buck of Bucksport* (Ellsworth, Me.: Ellsworth American, 1975).

R.H. Cohoon, "The Witch's Curse Fulfilled," *Sun-Up, Maine's Own Magazine* 7, no. 1 (January 1929).

Collected Poems of Robert P. Tristram Coffin (New York: Macmillan, 1948).

Alpheus Hyatt Verrill, *Romantic and Historic Maine* (New York: Dodd, Mead & Co., 1933).

"The Haunted Isles"

Horace Palmer Beck, *Folklore of Maine* (Philadelphia: Lippincott, 1957).

Marie Donahue, "Celia Thaxter's Island World," *Down East* (August 1976).

John Scribner Jenness, *The Isles of Shoals* (Hanover, N.H.: Peter E. Randall, 1975).

"Romance and Grim Tragedy Stalk Barren Rocky Shores of Desolate Isles of Shoals," *Portland Sunday Telegram* (5 March 1933).

Lyman V. Rutledge, *The Isles of Shoals in Lore and Legend* (Barre, Mass.: Barre Publishers, 1965).

Captain John Smith, *Description of New England*, Old South Leaflets 5, Resource and Source Work Series #106 (New York: Burt Franklin), pps. 101–25.

Acknowledgments and Sources

Celia Thaxter, *Among the Isles of Shoals* (Boston: Houghton Mifflin Co, 1873).

"Pirate Ghosts and Haunted Caves"

William Hayes, *Casco Bay Yarns* (New York: D.O. Haynes & Co., 1916).

Herbert G. Jones, *The Isles of Casco Bay in Fact and Fancy* (Freeport, Me.: Bond Wheelwright Co., 1946).

Hazel S. Loveitt, "Did Pirate Ann Bonney Dig Those Seven Graves?" (Portland) *Evening Express* (10 January 1969).

Theodore J. Morrill, "Pirate Gold Is Sought on Jewell Island in Casco Bay, *Portland Sunday Telegram* (3 September 1939).

Dorothy Simpson, *The Maine Islands in Story and Legend* (Philadelphia: Lippincott, 1960).

"The Lingering Soul of Father Moriarty"

Henry Gosselin, "Is Father Moriarty's Spirit Roaming in the Old Brewer Rectory?" *The Church World, Maine's Catholic Weekly* (28 October 1976).

"The Woman In the Shawl"

Myrtle Kitteridge Lovejoy, *This Was Stroudwater* (National Society of Colonial Dames of America in the State of Maine, 1985).

"The Ghost in the Cellar"

"Will Begin Life Anew. William E. Gould Released from Confinement," (Portland) *Eastern Argus* (1 October 1891).

Obituary of William E. Gould, *Portland Daily Press* (17 April 1919).

"The Footless Ghost of Benton Falls"

Paul Downing, "Does a Ghost Go With the Bones?" *Maine Sunday Telegram* (16 August 1970).

Ibid., "Things Go Bump in the Night," *Maine Sunday Telegram* (30 August 1970).

Ibid., "The Strange Saga of Benton Falls," *Maine Sunday Telegram* (25 October 1970).

"The Chinese Curse of Naples"

Robert Jordan Dingley, *Now I Will Tell You—Story of Naples* (Naples, Maine, Historical Society, 1979).

Obituary of Charles R. White, *Portland Press Herald* (10 July 1931).

"Serenity Hill Curse Defied by Widow," *Portland Sunday Telegram* (26 July 1953).

Geoffrey C. Ward and Frederic Delano Grant, Jr., "A Fair, Honorable, and Legitimate Trade," American Heritage 37 (August/September 1986).

"The Haunted Castle"

Sylvester B. Beckett, *Hester, The Bride of the Islands: A Poem* (Portland, Me.: Bailey & Noyes, 1860).

Lynne Campbell, "Footsteps from the Past," *Portland Chronicle* 2, no. 8 (29 December 1982–12 January 1983).

Arthur Myers, *The Ghostly Register* (Chicago: Contemporary Books, 1986).

Obituary of Sylvester B. Beckett, (Portland) *Eastern Argus* (4 December 1882).

Twenty-Third Annual Report of the Proceedings of the Maine Press Association for the Year Ending February 1, 1886 (Bar Harbor, Me.: Mount Desert Publishing Company, 1886).

"The Dagger and the Chair"

Obituary of Robert W. Plant, *Portland Press Herald* (14 October 1940).

"The Ghost in the Aisles"

Michael Kimball, "Searching for Voices from the 'Other Side,' " *Yankee* 48, no. 11 (November 1984).

Myers, *The Ghostly Register,* op. cit.

"The Ghostly Campus"

Ira Glackens, *Yankee Diva,* (New York: Coleridge Press, 1963).

Maine Stream (student publication, University of Maine at Farmington) 6, no. 4 (26 October 1979).

Richard P. Mallett, *University of Maine at Farmington* (Freeport, Me.: Bond Wheelwright Co., 1974).

Acknowledgments and Sources

"The Haunted Tavern of Freeport"

William D. Barry, "Reassessing the Freeport Massacre," (Brunswick) *Times Record* (12 October 1978).

Sheldon Christian, "Means Massacre at Flying Point Is One of Maine's Famous Tales," *Lewiston Journal* (22 April 1964).

Charles Parker Ilsley, *The Canadian Captive* (Freeport, Me.: Freeport Press, 1932).

"Two Centuries of Freeport's History. Part of Yarmouth Called Harraseeket" *Lewiston Journal* (20–23 April, 1910).

Verrill, *Romantic and Historic Maine*, op. cit.

"The Portrait of a Lady"

Rick Litchfield, *The Captain Lord Mansion—An Abbvreviated History* (pamphlet).

The Ghostly Night Watchman"

Joyce Butler, "Silas Perkins: Kennebunkport's Philosopher of the Coal Wharf," *Bittersweet* (April 1984).

Tony Labonte, Richard Obrey, and Thomas A. Verde, "Mysteries of Maine" (video presentation of Dunn and Sons Productions and Xavier Corporation, © 1987. Executive Producer William J. Dunn).

Myers, *The Ghostly Register*, op. cit.

With grateful appreciation, the author also wishes to acknowledge his indebtedness to the following institutions and individuals who made the writing of this book a possibility: The Maine Historical Society; The Portland Room, Portland Public Library; The Freeport Historical Society; The B.H. Bartol Library (Freeport); Naples Town Hall; The McArthur Library (Biddeford); The University of Maine at Farmington; The Nordica Homestead Museum; Joel Eastman, Loren Coleman and Alex Tanous for their guidance; Karin Womer and Julie Fallowfield for their patience; and Clare Casey for all that and more.

Also thanks go to Kelly, Sven, Brenda, Monte, and Tricia for letting me use their cars; to Dave, for letting me use his couch; and to *Casco Bay Weekly* for the time and the tube.